POSITIONING
YOURSELF TO BE A

Wife

THE ULTIMATE GUIDE FOR
YOUR FIRST AND ONLY MARRIAGE

SHAMIEKA DEAN

Positioning Yourself to be a Wife
The Ultimate Guide for Your First and Only Marriage

Dean Productions, LLC
Clarksville, TN 37042

ISBN: 978-0-9977065-0-5

Printed in the United States of America

Dedication

First and always, I thank God for giving me the strength, courage, and wisdom to write this book. This book has been one of purging, healing, and breakthrough—even for me. There were many days I wanted to say no to this book, as it describes very intimate details of my flaws, but God's perfect grace. I have cried many times throughout this process, but I know that although it's my story, it's for His glory.

My king, Parnell Dean, you are beyond amazing. There are times when I literally cry crocodile tears wondering how and why God gave me you, someone who loves me as unconditionally and intensely as you do. A man who supports my dreams even when they don't make sense to me. A man who provides, protects, and cares for me with such thoughtfulness. A man who loved me when I was unlovable. The only man other than God who can calm my storm and bring peace to my chaos. I know I wrote the vision and made it plain, but you're the evidence of Ephesians 3:20. You are far more exceedingly abundantly above all that I could ask or think. I asked for the bare minimum in a husband but with you, God gave me more than enough. You're a rare breed my king, and I love you immensely.

My children: Terrishiell, Emmanuel, and Orlando, thanks for allowing Mommy to have her moments of silence and struggle to produce this life-changing book. You all have been a constant inspiration to me. The times when I wanted to quit I remembered the promise I made to you all of leaving a legacy of greatness. Greatness requires completing what you've started and doing what you need to do even when you don't feel like it. Thanks for your patience, kisses, warm hugs, and continuous words of encouragement. Terrishiell, I'm calling you out to finish your book next.

To contributing author Courtney Aiken, my life has been forever changed for the better since God allowed us to cross paths. You're a gem, and I'm honored to have your words of wisdom added to this life-changing book.

My friends, family, and supporters, I want to thank you for holding me accountable. Thanks for sharing your relationship successes with me. Many times your testimonies of how my wisdom has helped you in your relationship gave me the push I needed to write another chapter. I wholeheartedly believe that this masterpiece is one that you can utilize no matter where you are in your relationship. I appreciate you for believing in the gift that God has placed within me.

Contents

Introduction

On February 14, 2012 (Valentine's Day), with the sun shining brightly and the wind blowing softly, I hovered my hand over my eyes to block the sun as I walked to the black mailbox painted with the gold numbers 3316. I began sorting through the mail. As usual—junk mail, a sales paper, and bills, but then I got to the big, white envelope and that nauseating feeling came again—the feeling confirming my reality. Following the nausea was the knot in my throat from fighting back tears, and the thought of allowing myself to fall knees first into the concrete curb underneath me. I was taught to always prepare for the worst, but let me assure you from experience that you cannot prepare for the day you'll have to pick up the millions of pieces of your shattered heart. I knew this day was coming. But nothing could prepare me for this overwhelming pain that would take over my entire being the moment I opened the big, white envelope to read what I had been dreading for almost a year. I opened the envelope, unfolded the papers, and right across the top in big, bold letters it read: FINAL DISSOLUTION OF MARRIAGE!

The pain, the anger, the disappointment, and the gut-wrenching feeling had smothered me. It was official. I was a divorcee with three kids. I never imagined after being married for only seven years to the man I thought I would grow old with, that I would divorce. NOW WHAT?! I proceeded to walk into the house. I felt numb all over, wanting to scream and cry. My emotions were all over the place. My legs began to feel heavier with each step. When I finally made it to the top of the steps, I fell to my knees crying out to God. I asked, "How did I get here?" He responded, "Because you were a single-married woman. The only thing that changed when you said, 'I do' was your last name."

. . . .

SINGLE-MARRIED WOMAN—*a woman who is married but has the heart, mind, and actions of a single woman.*

. . . .

This is exactly who I was. I said, "I do" but I was not a wife. My divorce changed my life and the process I went through following my divorce positioned me to be a wife. During the five months my husband and I were divorced, God showed me the true definition of what it means to be a wife. A wife is more than a title. It is a position of influence, strength, and power. When I first started writing this book, my intention was to write it for married women. However, God said, "I want you to write it from where you were as a single-married woman." There are so many things we do not prepare for when it comes to marriage. We prepare for the wedding, honeymoon, and the reception, but not to become a wife.

This book will take you through the process I went through during my divorce that positioned me to be a wife. *Positioning Yourself to be a Wife* will take you through a three-step process, which is to purge, prepare, and position. The process will *purge* you from what's hindering you from getting to the altar, *prepare* you for the man and marriage you've been praying for, and *position* you as a wife to be found by your king. *Positioning Yourself to be a Wife* serves as a guide for preparation, prevention, and sustainability to women who desire to get married and stay married. These are things I wish I had known before I got married and things that could've been prevented had I positioned myself to be a wife.

Singlehood has been determined by society as almost a plague. When a woman says she's single, people automatically think something is wrong with her. This has caused many women to desperately desire marriage for all of the wrong reasons. Marriage won't cure your loneliness or heal your brokenness. Being single is a time of exploration, revelation, and preparation. This is the time when you explore the depth of who you are and the value you possess. You receive revelation about the hidden things hindering you from receiving the love you deserve and desire, and going through the process to prepare for your happy marriage.

Purge

$\mathcal{T}$he first step in the process is to purge. Purging is a process to remove anything that is unwanted, impure, or undesirable; to cleanse or purify. This process consists of finding and destroying the root issues in your life that are preventing you from accessing your position or will cause you to lose your position. In order to destroy the root, you have to know where it started which is why the very first step in *Positioning Yourself to be a Wife* is revisiting the pain that got you here.

Revisit the Pain

In my search to heal from the aftermath of a divorce, I was led to the fascinating story in the Bible about a Queen named Esther. Queen Esther was a Jewish orphan who became the queen who replaced the position of Queen Vashti. Queen Vashti lost her position because of her refusal to adhere to the request of King Xerxes when he requested her presence. We'll talk more about Queen Vashti in "Playing Your Position To Win." The backstory of Queen Esther is that she was a Jewish orphan raised by her cousin Mordecai after their family had been exiled from Jerusalem.

Before Queen Esther took her position as Queen, she had to go through a purification process to prepare for her position. It was a twelve-month process that consisted of being bathed and soaked in oil of myrrh the first six months, and being bathed in sweet smelling fragrances the next six months. I want to highlight the oil of myrrh. Oil of myrrh is used for things such as anti-fungal, yeast infections, and ringworms, but most importantly, it was used to heal wounds. What wounds could a Jewish virgin girl possibly have? Let's put ourselves in Queen Esther's shoes for a minute. She had been abandoned due to the death of her parents. She was kicked out of her country. It doesn't state exactly how old she was, but she must've been young since her cousin Mordecai had to raise her; therefore, she didn't know who she was because everything and everyone who was supposed to teach her that, she had been separated from.

Queen Esther's wounds could easily be identified as abandonment issues, rejection issues, and identity issues. These wounds would certainly affect her position as queen. Queen Esther had to be healed from the wounds of her past that could contaminate her king, cost her her position, or abort the mission God had for her marriage to King Xerxes. After the healing process with the oil of myrrh, she was sprayed outwardly, beautified and covered with the sweet smelling fragrances. Notice that she wasn't beautified outwardly with the sweet smelling fragrances until she had been healed inwardly, because covering up internal wounds will only suppress them. Eventually those wounds will rise to the surface and the longer the wound remains unhealed, the more damage it will cost.

Reading the story of Queen Esther reminded me so much of myself. I too grew up with abandonment issues, rejections issues, and identity issues. I had practiced covering up my wounds with false confidence and strength for years. Eventually, it all rose to the surface that cost my marriage. I didn't realize I had so many unresolved issues in my heart. I thought that I had healed from my issues since I had moved forward in life and forgiven people. The truth is, although I had moved on in life, the aftermath hadn't been dealt with. An open wound is very hard to heal when it's covered. Bitterness is one of those things that is so easy to take root when unforgiveness is in your heart. Bitterness had taken root in my heart, and it reflected in my actions toward my husband. Parnell and I got married less than three months of meeting. In our efforts to have a happy marriage, we never completely opened up to each other the way we should have. There were so many things we overlooked all for the sake of staying married.

We were living under the same roof and doing things married couples do, but the wounds were deep. We did what most people do; we just moved forward. We had suppressed our pain, never addressing the issues, or getting to the root of anything. If it's one thing I've learned from our story, it's that ignoring a problem doesn't solve it. If anything, it makes it worse as time goes on. Unfortunately, we didn't take the time to assess or address what we had gone through. We didn't have that type of wisdom back then to learn anything from what we had gone through. We were fighting hard to stay together only to constantly drift apart. My language toward him became more and more harsh, and his disrespect toward me became normal. He had built up resentment in his heart toward me. There came a point where I found more peace away from him than around him. The feelings were mutual because he would get off of work, go by the liquor store and come home, only to sit in his car for hours until it was time for him to go to bed. This behavior began to disgust me, and the man I loved was turning into the man I despised.

My affection toward him was already slim, but it became less and less. This was a huge problem for him because like most men they assume it has to be another man getting what we aren't giving them. Accusations started flying and tempers were at an all-time high. I saw changes in my husband that I hadn't seen before. At the time, I didn't know that he was suffering horribly from post-traumatic stress syndrome or PTSD. If you've ever dealt with someone who had PTSD, you would understand just how bad it can get. The fear and paranoia they go through at times is almost unbearable to deal with. All of the issues facing us would soon be intensified due to an upcoming deployment. We mustered up the strength to stay on decent terms to try to get through the deployment, but it wasn't enough. So much damage had been done. We were barely talking when he was deployed, but when we did talk, we ended up arguing for the most part. We were even arguing through email.

I remember receiving an email saying he wanted a divorce, and I couldn't believe it. I was at the end of my rope, so I told him to do what he had to do. Here we were again going through another divorce conversation. Of course I was oblivious to the fact that he was actually serious this time. It wasn't until I got the divorce decree in the mail that I realized he was serious. It was so hard to believe that this was what he really wanted because one day he would be talking like we were husband and wife, and the next minute he would treat me like an enemy. I was confused day to day. He even came home for R & R (rest and recuperation) like everything was fine. He would still tell me he loved me, and sent whatever I needed when I needed it. I assumed things were okay but little did I know, he was still planning to proceed with the divorce. The love in me wanted to fight for our marriage, but the pride in me gave him what he asked for. I signed the papers and continued life as usual. Heartbroken to say the least, but also determined to move on with my life.

March 2012, I was headed to Arkansas for my son's grandfather's funeral, who had succumbed to cancer, when I was caught in a tornado that caused injuries to my spine. My spine was actually pushed and curved to the right. The pain had become so unbearable I couldn't do anything for myself. I was in pain and in tears because I felt so helpless.

My ex-husband had come to get the kids that weekend. I was in so much pain, I couldn't even walk the kids to the door. He ended up coming in and the kids told him what happened. He told me that he would stay to help take care of me until I could take care of myself. I initially refused; however, I had no one else to help me. I couldn't even bathe myself. The house we lived in had a bonus room connected to the back of the house. He bought an air mattress and stayed in the back room so that he could nurse me back to health. He bathed me, and he cooked every day. He took care of everything the kids needed. He had been staying with a friend until he could save up to get his own apartment but felt he was overstaying his welcome. He asked me if he could pay my rent to stay in the bonus room until he got his apartment. I agreed.

He did his part in helping out in the house and with the kids. After being there for about two weeks, he came into my room one night to talk. He asked if I had ever thought about us getting back together. I told him that I did, but I needed time to think. He said he understood. He then asked if we could at least be friends. I told him that we could. One day my youngest son said, "Daddy, is Mommy still beautiful to you? You always said Mommy was beautiful." Turning to look into my eyes, he responded, "Yes she is. She's always been beautiful and she still is." Well, since she's still beautiful, why don't you take her on a date and maybe she can be your wife again?" I couldn't believe my son was trying to play matchmaker. My ex-husband decided to take his advice and asked me if I wanted to go get something to eat. He knows that food is the way to my heart.

The date started out a little awkward, but soon we were laughing and talking about the good ol' days. The date was fun; the night ended well. I felt myself feeling something for him I hadn't felt in a long time. When he would grab my hand during our date, I felt like a school-age girl on a date with her biggest crush. It was so different. I think it was that moment I realized that he was changing. It was the way he handled me with such care. The tone of his voice when he said, "Shamieka, I still love you." The look in his eyes when he told me I was beautiful. The way he grabbed my hand to walk me into the restaurant. When we returned home that night, he said, "If I ever get a chance to make you my wife again, I'll do everything in my power to keep you happy. I know I messed up," he continued, "I also know you're my wife, and I'm trusting God to help me get you back in my life." I did all that I could to hold back the tears. I quickly turned my head and walked away in silence. I didn't have the courage to respond because in my heart, the marriage was over.

When the divorce became a reality, one of the first things I asked God was how did we get here. I needed to know this because the pain of divorce was one of the most intense pains I had ever experienced in my life. I never wanted to experience that type of pain again, and wanted to learn from this mistake once and for all. My immediate thoughts went to what had transpired over the past year and a half, but God revealed to me that the problems in my marriage started long before I said, "I do." My issues started in childhood. Things I assumed I had overcome, I found out I had only suppressed. What's in you will come out. It's only a matter of time for the right situation to present itself. I brought a lot of baggage into my marriage and all of these things played a huge factor in how my husband and I got to divorce court.

Assuming that your current situation is a result of "current issues" is more than likely not the case. We often think that the current situation is what got us to this place, failing to realize that we never emptied the garbage of our childhood or past relationships. When dealing with matters of the heart, you have to go backwards before you can move forward. That's exactly what I had to do so I wouldn't end up in divorce court again. God challenged everything within me. He made me evaluate my thinking as well as my actions.

- *Why did I think the way I thought toward men?*
- *Why did I act the way I acted toward men?*
- *Why did I communicate the way I did?*
- *Why did I have the fears I had regarding men and marriage?*

Every stone had to be unturned if I didn't want to go on this merry-go-round of divorce again. I began traveling down memory lane, revisiting the pain that got me here. This journey wasn't easy for me and as you read the next few paragraphs, you'll see why.

Sound asleep in a queen-size bed, I felt the cool air hit my body and a slight tug on my arm. Fear struck me because I thought it was the Boogeyman from the movie I had watched around 7 p.m. earlier that night. I rubbed my eyes to see which way I needed to run, but was comforted to open my eyes and see that it was someone I knew. He whispered, "Come here. I have to show you something." I got up in my soft pink cotton nightgown with a white-laced circle patch underneath my neck that had a pink bow on it. I followed his lead into his bedroom where his queen-size bed was sitting horizontally up against the wall.

Right next to it was the bench, the black, cold leather weight bench that ruined my life. I will never forget how cold it was pressed against my back as he lifted my pink nightgown and slid down my white cotton underwear with the word *Tuesday* written in blue letters. Even at ten years old, I knew this wasn't right. "Shhh! Just be still. Don't say nothing. I promise it won't hurt," were the words from his mouth. "I'm going to buy you something if you be real quiet." Then he placed one hand over my mouth as he dropped his basketball shorts and penetrated my ten-year-old vagina with his eighteen-year-old penis. Confused and in pain, I began to whimper until he was done. He grabbed me by the hand, pulled me up off of the bench, and walked me into the bathroom. I will never forget the cold, white floor and flowered wallpaper as I looked into the mirror while he cleaned me with a cold, wet towel. Then he said three words that made me sick to my stomach: I love you. He tip-toed me back into the bedroom where he found me and helped me get back into bed whispering, "You can't ever tell anybody. If you do, I will have to hurt you and your family." My mind flooded with thoughts. *Why does this sound so familiar? Were they talking to each other about me? How did he know to do to me the same thing the other one had done? This is a different person, different place, different time, but they said almost the same thing. Why is this happening to me again? What is wrong with me that I deserved this?*

I was home from school that day, walking through the house on my way to the kitchen when the phone rang. On the other end, a family member asked, "Do you all have some sugar?" I replied, "Yes." He said, "I need to come over and get it. Are you home alone? Where is your mom and dad?" I told him they were at work, and he proceeded to come over. When he came to the house, I opened the door without hesitation because he was family. I went to get the sugar with him following close behind me. He acted as if he was heading to the door to leave, so I went into my mother's room to put the remote up because I had been cleaning up. And out of nowhere, he appeared. He told me he needed to do something that would make me feel good and told me to lay on the bed because he needed to show me something. I did as I was instructed to by this fourteen-year-old. He then grabbed my hands with one of his, placing them over my head as he pulled his pants down. He then pulled my pants down and away went my innocence. "You better not tell anyone or I will kill you," he told me. "No one would believe you anyway." I didn't scream. I didn't yell. I knew it felt wrong, but I didn't understand it or know what to do.

In that moment, he not only took away my innocence, but he took away my VOICE and my ability to fight back! My dad walked into the house, which startled him causing him to run out the back door. He asked me what happened and I explained the best I could. He called my mom and she came home furious. I was drilled and grilled with so many questions. I expected my mom to comfort me, but instead I was whooped and told I shouldn't have opened the door.

When this second rape happened two months later by a different individual who was eighteen, I didn't tell anyone until I turned twenty-one years old. I lived with that guilt for years. I felt like I deserved the second one since I opened the door and I allowed the first one to happen. I had no safety net. Who could I turn to if my own mother wouldn't protect me? I was angry at myself for years because I thought that maybe if I said, "Stop!" he wouldn't have done it. I thought, *Why didn't you fight him off, Shamieka?*

These men took away my voice, my identity and left me feeling hopeless, damaged, and broken. They violated my trust. The one I trusted to comfort me abandoned me in that moment. I was left to heal from this on my own. Long before my divorce, I had issues that would ultimately help lead to the destruction of my marriage. As you can see from my story, I had a very good reason to have issues. One of the issues was with trust. My trust issues were deeper than just people. This incident caused a distrust with God. How could I trust God when He didn't protect me? Where was He when these males violated me? Why did He allow this to happen to me? The only example I had of love was associated with intense pain. The rapes, the rejection, the abuse, and the betrayal were all from people I loved and trusted. Everyone I gave my all to destroyed me and little by little, a piece of my heart was chipped away by each of them.

My vision of love was warped by people who didn't know how to love me. There were also the "credible" voices in my life that directly impacted my image of men and relationships. Growing up, I was told things like, "Don't trust no man." "These men ain't no good." "If you can't beat them, join them." "What's good for the goose is good for the gander." Because I valued the people who taught me this, their words were a part of what shaped my world. I adapted to *their* way of thinking and applied it to my life. I didn't understand the impact of that mentality until God had me to carefully evaluate everything I had been taught. As much as you value the wisdom of those people in your life who are "credible," you have to make sure that what you've been taught will help you and not hinder you. Carefully evaluate the things you've been taught and the impact of the tragedies that have happened to you. These things may be causing you to build up a wall of trust issues or even negative images of men and marriage. I realized after revisiting my pain that I lacked confidence, struggled with fear, and harbored resentment, bitterness, and unforgiveness in my heart.

In *Positioning Yourself to be a Wife*, you have to figure out what got you to this place. This process is not going to be easy. There will be times when you want to revert to your comfort zone, but in order to have the type of love your heart longs for, this process must be completed.

- *Why do you think the way that you think about men or marriage?*
- *Why do you think the way you think, period?*
- *Are your thought patterns based on what you were taught by the credible people in your life like your mom, grandmother, father, friends, or pastor?*

Think about the significant events that happened in your life that caused you to have the mindset you have now regarding relationships. I want you to really think about those most impactful moments in your life. Think about your relationship with your parents, childhood friends, high school peers, teachers, and preachers. Are there any tragedies such as rape, abuse, abandonment, or rejection that are causing you to have trust issues with men? What were the words the credible people in your life said to you? Do these words or thinking line up with the word of God?

Take out a notebook, write down the first words that come to mind and any negative emotions you feel when you think of love, relationships, or marriage. Ask God to reveal to you the incidents that have negatively impacted your view of love, men, or marriage.

Take Your Power Back

Once you've revisited the pain that got you to this place and discovered the "why" behind your actions, it's time to take your power back. In order to take your power back, you have to forgive. One of the steps in the healing process is forgiveness. Attempting to bypass forgiveness is like putting clean clothes on a dirty body. You'll contaminate the new clothes with the old dirt. Without forgiveness, your healing process is incomplete and you'll take that old hurt into your new relationship.

What is forgiveness? Forgiveness is POWER! It is power to take back everything that was taken from you in that broken relationship, childhood pain, rejection, or any other instance that caused you heartache. It is power to take back your identity, your voice, and your worth. It is power to take your happiness out of the hands of the person who tried to destroy it. Forgiveness is not a feeling. The truth is, you may not ever feel like forgiving them, and your feelings will always give you a reason to justify your decision to not forgive. But the longer you hold on to unforgiveness, the longer you'll remain in pain. Forgiveness is also a CHOICE. A choice to heal even if you never get the apology you deserve. A choice to heal even if they never change their actions that caused you the pain. A choice to heal even when it hurts. Forgiveness is a nonnegotiable part of the healing process. Forgiveness is strength because it takes a strong person to forgive someone who has betrayed him or her. You may feel like you can't forgive. I used to think the same thing but God will never tell you to do anything that He hasn't equipped you to do. You can do all things through Christ who strengthens you (Philippians 4:13), including forgive those who hurt you. Without forgiveness, you can move forward, but you will not be able to move on. Forgiveness has never been about the offender, but it will always be about you. You don't forgive them because they deserve it. You forgive them because *you* deserve it. You deserve to be healed.

I wish I had understood forgiveness earlier in life, because it took me years to take my power back. It wasn't until 2007 that I learned the power of forgiveness through my relationship with my biological father. Sitting on the edge of my bed, my face soaked with tears, I screamed to the top of my lungs, "Where were you when I needed you? Where were you when I needed you to protect me from the men who raped me? Why did you not love me enough to be in my life? What is wrong with me? Am I too ugly for you to love me? Am I unlovable? All I wanted was to have the privilege of being daddy's little girl." These were the words of a fatherless child. A young woman who so desperately needed her father to be in her life. A young woman who couldn't understand what she did to deserve rejection by her own father. These were my words. These were the words I cried out to God trying to figure out what was it about me that made my own father choose not to love me.

For twenty-five years, I was so angry with him. I blamed him for my choices in life and blamed him for my rapes, believing if he had been there, none of those things would've happened. I recall seeing him and my brother at a store one day. It was like interacting with a stranger. "Hi," he said. He seemed surprised and happy to see me, but I was not happy to see him at all. At this point in life, I didn't care if he existed. That's how much anger I had in my heart toward him. I responded, "Hi!" to my father and my brother got upset because I didn't stop to hold a conversation or acknowledge him. You're not going to stop and talk to your father?" he asked. "He's not my father," I replied. "He's your father. He's never done anything for me."

Every time I would see him, I would become consumed by anger because a part of me wanted my father to hurt the way he had hurt me. For part of my life I denied that he was my father, giving him a dose of his own medicine. I inflicted the pain of rejection on him, wanting him to feel the pain of rejection I had felt—thinking maybe it would compel him to be involved in my life. But no matter how much I tried to hurt him for hurting me, it didn't heal me. There were nights I would not allow myself to cry, because I felt that if I cried, it meant I cared about him. I didn't want to care for him because in my mind, he didn't care for me. The anger, bitterness, and pain radiated from me profusely.

My father lived two minutes driving distance away from me and never came to see me. I spent years trying to fill the void of my father by getting involved in relationships with men. I remember a feeling of sadness would overtake me when I went to my friends' houses and their fathers would be in the home. I would often visualize myself as my friend, trying to feel that fatherly love. The pain was so intense at times that my friends would ask me to come over, and I would make up an excuse not to go simply because I didn't want to be reminded of the void I felt in my heart.

The damage to my self-esteem and fear of rejection started with my father, but it was compounded by the rapes I went through. We look to men to protect us because we know that's what they are created to do. Fathers are the first man a girl falls in love with, even if the relationship is a toxic one. The relationship with her father sets the tone for how she perceives what a relationship with a man is supposed to be like. I wanted so badly for my father to love me and to be in my life. Even though he rejected me and his absence hurt me, I still longed for him. This set the tone for how I allowed men in relationships to treat me. Even when they hurt me, I longed for them. In my mind, if I could get just one to stay in my life, it would make me feel validated. It would make me feel like I was worthy of being loved and that my father was wrong. The constant rejection, failed relationships, and continual heartache made me feel like something had to be wrong with me.

In the midst of my tears that night I poured my heart out to God, I heard Him say, "Forgive him!" Confused by His response I replied, "Why should I forgive him after all he's done to me?" Feeling justified by my reasoning not to forgive, His response left me speechless. "I forgave you for all you've done. Love him for who he is, instead of hating him because he's not who you want him to be." After that, I knew I had to forgive my father.

It took me a while before I made a move. I didn't have the courage to tell my father how I felt face to face, so I wrote a letter and dropped it off to his wife since he wasn't home. A couple of days later, my children and I went by his house. His wife walked us into the bedroom where he was sitting with his long, gray, and wavy hair watching television. He looked up at me, smiled, and opened his arms for me to hug him. At age twenty-five, I hugged my father for the first time. This was the first time I had ever been this up close and personal to my father.

My children stood next to me, and we sat there quietly for about five minutes. He broke the awkward silence. "I got your letter." I said, "Okay," as silence filled the room again. I looked at him and tears slowly began to roll down his face. "I do love you." He continued, "I never came to you because I didn't think you would want me to. I didn't feel like I deserved to be in your life because I know I didn't do what I should've done." To hear my father say he loved me healed wounds that were deeply embedded in me for over twenty-five years. I cried as he held me in his arms, but this time these were tears of joy. In that moment, I completely forgave him.

In the letter I told him I wanted him to be there for my children. He promised to do so, and he kept that promise. He developed a relationship with my children that grew. He spoiled my children. In addition, I got to know my father as a very sweet, humble, and soft-spoken man who loved people and loved to crack jokes. If I had one regret, it would be choosing not to forgive him sooner because I missed out on so many years of knowing such a great man. That day I combed his beautiful hair for hours. We laughed. We bonded. But little did I know, my father was gravely ill at that time. He had been in and out of the hospital the last two years of his life and in November 2009, he passed away from pancreatic cancer. I am thankful for the opportunity to love him for who he was, and no longer hated him for who he was not. I did not have to live with the regret of not taking the opportunity to forgive him before he passed away.

Have you ever wondered why forgiveness is so difficult? I know it is difficult because of the heartache that is associated with it. It's difficult because of the one who hurt you and how they hurt you. But beyond that, why is it so difficult to forgive? I asked God. "Why is it so hard to forgive?" And He responded, "Why does the enemy make things hard for you?" I had a moment of revelation. The only time the enemy makes things difficult for us is when there is a blessing awaiting us. Let's look at one of my favorite scriptures.

"Bless the Lord, O my soul, and forget not all his bene-fits: Who forgiveth all thine iniquities; who healeth all thy diseases; Who redeemeth thy life from destruction; who crowneth thee with lovingkindness and tender mercies; Who satisfieth thy mouth with good things; so that thy youth is renewed like the eagle's."

PSALMS 103:2-5 KJV

Pay close attention to the order of this passage of scriptures. The first thing it talks about are the benefits. But what has to happen for you to have access to those benefits? Before we can have access to any of the promises of God, forgiveness of sins has to take place. Forgiveness opens the pathway to healing. Did you know that unforgiveness is a disease because it affects you? It puts your body at *dis*-ease. Even doctors have medically proven the negative affects and sicknesses that are caused by unforgiveness. When you are at dis-ease, it prevents you from enjoying the fullness of life. It hinders you, affecting your emotions and mind. Your thoughts become things, so if it affects your mind, it affects your life. If it affects your life, it will affect every relationship you're in.

Forgiveness opens the pathway to redemption. When you experience heartache, you go down into a pit of sadness. When I think of a pit, I envision it being the lowest of the low which can lead to depression, anger, bitterness, and rage. It's a place where nobody can bring you out of but God. When you choose to forgive the person who hurt you, you open up the door for God to bless you with good. Your choice to forgive allows God to renew your mind so that your old mindset won't corrupt your new relationship, ending up destroying it. It gives you the strength to close the door to the one who hurt you and makes room for the one who will know you completely, love you unconditionally, love you like Christ loves the church, and treat you like the Queen you are.

Breathe! I know! You will receive that same refreshing feeling of freedom, healing, and peace that comes when you forgive that I did when I understood the benefits of forgiveness. I know you're excited about forgiving, and you're ready to find out how because you want all of the benefits God has for you. Another reason it's so hard to forgive others is because you do not believe that God has truly forgiven you. It's very difficult to extend mercy, love, and grace toward others when you haven't taken the time to extend it to yourself whenever you've fallen short. Evaluate your heart. Ask God to show you if you've truly forgiven yourself. If you know you haven't forgiven yourself, this is the beginning of your healing process.

In Psalms 103:12 it says, "As far as the east is from the west so far does he removed our transgressions from us." He removed them from you as far as the east is from the west. They can't even reconnect themselves to you because Jesus has taken on those sins and paid the price for them. Isaiah 43:25 (NIV) reads "I, even I, am he who blots out your transgressions, for my own sake, and remembers your sins no more." If He chooses not to remember them anymore, He can't hold against you something He no longer remembers. If anyone does sin, any kind of sin, we have someone pleading to God, our Father, interceding on our behalf. Jesus Christ, our Redeemer, the Righteous One, and He is the propitiation for our sins. Propitiation means that which appeases His anger and brings reconciliation with someone who has reason to be angry with someone else for our sins. In other words, He satisfies the debt to God for our sins and God's anger toward us to bring us back into the right relationship with God. "And not only for our sins, but for the sins of the world." (1 John 2: 2-3)

"The law was brought in so that the trespass might increase. But where sin increased, grace increased all the more, This is so refreshing because that means your sin can't outweigh God's grace. Grace covered it because it is by grace through faith that we are saved!" Lastly, Romans 8:1 (NKJV) says, "There is therefore now no condemnation to those who are in Christ Jesus,[a] who do not walk according to the flesh, but according to the Spirit."

ROMANS 5:20 (NIV)

Understand that God is not consistently reminding you of your sins, making you feel guilty, or waiting to punish you for your sins because the price has already been paid. If your thoughts are not pointing you toward God's love, grace, and mercy whenever you've fallen short, then that is the enemy trying to keep you in bondage. You have to fight back using your power which is the word of God. When you are reminded of your sins, remind yourself that you are forgiven, and let the enemy know that you're forgiven because grace covered it. Don't hold yourself hostage to anything God has forgiven you for.

When you understand the depth of your own sins, but most importantly, the depth of God's love and mercy for you, compassion will begin to fill your heart making it easier for you to forgive the ones who hurt you. If you are like me, I knew all of this stuff about forgiveness, yet there were still some wounds that were too deep for me to forgive. I would tell God when a person was too hard for me to forgive, and I would hear Him clearly say, "Forgive them for they know not what they do." I was confused, thinking *How can they possibly not know what they did when I told them and they saw my tears?* He said, "They know what they did, but they didn't understand who they did it to."

Most of the time, the ones who hurt us are the ones we are called to help. We have what that person needs to help them heal from their hurt. I'm sure you've heard the saying, "Hurt people, hurt people." I thought that was a bunch of malarkey, but it is one of the truest statements I've ever heard. I was a broken young woman who reproduced that same brokenness in my life. It came out in my attitude, quick temper, sarcastic personality, self-destructing patterns, and intimidating behavior. God was placing people in my life to help me heal, but I was so broken that I pushed them away. I had suffered from rejection so much, I became the rejecter. *Forgive them for they know not what they do.* But some people like brokenness because it gets them the attention they long for. In this case, it is not you they are pushing away; it is their own healing they are pushing away.

How to Forgive

1. *Choose to forgive.* Every time you think about it, choose to forgive.
2. *Forgive yourself.* Remember, you did what you did based on where you were at that point in your life. God doesn't forgive you based on if you deserve it or not. He forgives you because He loves you. It is difficult to forgive others when you haven't learned how to forgive yourself.
3. *Accept responsibility.* Accept responsibility for your choices in response to what happened, and what you allowed regardless of why you allowed it. We can't control what others do, but we can choose how we respond. If you continue to put that responsibility for your decision in someone else's hands, you give them the power to control your happiness.
4. *Pray for those who hurt you.* This is difficult in the beginning, but when you're able to freely pray for those who hurt you, they no longer have power over you.

You'll know you have forgiven when you do not seek retaliation or revenge, or when you can think of them without any negative feelings being associated with it. When you can pray for them freely and earnestly, and bless those who spitefully misuse you, you have forgiven.

Tear Down The Walls

My husband honestly didn't have a fair chance from the jump. Past relationships caused me to become overly suspicious of any and everyone I met. In my mind, the world was against me. If you were nice to me, I believed you had an ulterior motive. I never dealt with those trust issues like I should've before I said, "I do." I had a deeply-rooted fear of being cheated on. I never believed that I was good enough for a man to be faithful to me. Every relationship I was in ended because of cheating. Every time I was cheated on, I attached it to my identity. It had to be something wrong with me as to why men kept doing this to me. For me, cheating is rejection. Whenever you're rejected in any way, you can easily allow this rejection to become your identity.

I was suspicious even if my husband had taken too long to call me. One night his father called him and wanted to hang out. I thought he was lying about it at first; however, his father called to assure me that they were together. My cousin had even let me know that he saw my husband in his hometown with his father. My husband told me he would be home around midnight, but when the clock struck twelve, I was boiling because he hadn't come home yet. I decided not to call his phone because in my mind he was out with some woman, and it would probably confirm what I had already feared. He finally rolled into the house around four o'clock that morning and when he did, he was wreaking alcohol. Here's a little information about me if you haven't figured it out yet: I was a fighter. When you hurt me, I fought. When he walked into the house, I asked him where he'd been. He said he was hanging out with his father, and around midnight he was about to take his father home, but he wasn't ready to go home. He continued explaining how his father asked him to take him to the casino for an hour. Since he hadn't really spent time with his father in a while, he decided to go ahead and do so. His story did not satisfy me and before I knew it, out of nowhere, I had punched him in the ear. He grabbed me and pushed me against the wall to restrain me. He was holding me with one hand as I continued to throw blow after blow. Terror gripped me when I watched him grab his right ear because as he unfolded his hand, it was full of blood. I hit him so hard in my rage that I burst his ear. Blood was pouring down the side of his face. I had hit him in the past, but never had I caused damage like this. *He's going to kill me*, I thought. His eyes enlarged to what looked like the size of golf balls as he glared at me with rage followed by unbelief and sadness. He sternly said to me, "You will not turn me into that guy. I have never hit a woman, and I never will. This is your last time putting your hands on me. If you ever hit me again, I will leave and never come back."

Although I knew he was serious, my pride wouldn't let me show any sign of weakness. I remained in my hostile, irrational position. I didn't hit him again, but I told him to get out. He promised me that he was telling the truth. He even told me to call his father, but I was so upset, I refused. That night I slept in the room with the kids. The next morning, I got up to clean our bedroom and grabbed his pants off of the floor to take them to the laundry room. A receipt fell out of his pocket. I picked it up, and it was a receipt with the casino time stamped to match his story. Not only that, his father's wife called his phone about an hour later yelling at him for keeping his father out until after almost four o'clock in the morning. I felt horrible. That was the beginning revelation of just how deep my trust issues were.

A person who doesn't trust anyone is a person who will attract people who will break their trust. If you want to break that cycle, you have to tear down those walls. The wall that has been built as a defense mechanism is also keeping you in bondage. Trust issues are rooted in fear, which we will discuss in the next chapter.

Face Your Fear

With tumultuous relationships and childhood tragedies, pain can become your norm. When pain is all you've known, it can become your comfort zone and when you're comfortable, you won't make the necessary moves even if those moves will prove to be better for you. When pain becomes your home, fear becomes your friend and healing becomes your enemy. Fear can be so deeply embedded in you that you will subconsciously push away what you've been praying for.

Fear is a feeling, which means you can change it. When fear rises, you can either flee from it or face it. Fear doesn't simply go away. It has to be defeated with continuous action. If you are serious about *Positioning Yourself to Be a Wife*, defeating fear is a mandate, not an option. Fear has many masks that pretend to be strength and confidence until the masks are pulled off. Most women have masqueraded fear for so many years with pro-woman antics, alpha-female labels, intimidation, controlling behaviors, or nonchalant attitudes. Some women even try to disconnect emotionally by sleeping with multiple men, adopting the attitude and behaviors of some men. When you begin to pull back the layers, most of it is rooted in fear. Somewhere along the road someone hurt that woman, and she's lived a life to protect her heart from ever experiencing that type of pain again. However, it doesn't work. It really prevents her from experiencing the true love her heart so desires, because her walls won't allow anyone to get close enough to her to show her the love she desires. I know because I was one of those women.

I did it all. I was the face of the strong, black independent woman, always in control of my relationships. A man didn't stand a chance with me because of my controlling attitude and unwillingness to let them in. Every relationship left me broken, crying, and praying to God for someone to love me and treat me right. I was so afraid of getting hurt that when love found me, I was pushing it away—pushing away my promise because I was being ruled by fear. This is how I realized that I was masquerading fear. During our dating phase, my husband, Parnell and I were sitting on the couch one day when he pulled me close to him. Without thinking, I moved his hand away from me, but he pulled me closer. Again, I subconsciously pushed him away. He grabbed my face, looked me right in my eyes and said, "Will you please just let me love you?" Before I knew it, tears had begun to run down my face. I was crying uncontrollably as he laid my head gently on his shoulders. "I'm sorry. I don't know how," I said, finally explaining my actions. "I want to let you in, but I'm so scared because every man I've ever loved has hurt me, including my own father." Here I was with a man that was trying to love me but because I was so afraid of getting hurt by him, I was pushing him away. I had been let down by every man that came into my life, so I assumed he would do it too. I wanted to be loved, but I didn't know how because fear was my ruler.

Take a deep look at your thoughts and actions. What fears are you masquerading? Some of the most common fears that most single women face are:

- *Fear of never getting married*
- *Fear of not being good enough*
- *Fear of divorce*
- *Fear of the unknown (What is marriage all about?)*

These fears are based on history and surroundings. The feeling of unworthiness is rooted in a lack of confidence or the fear of rejection due to being abandoned or rejected in the past. If all of your past relationships ended because of cheating, you'll develop a fear that it will happen again. The media paints a pretty gloomy picture of marriage. The divorce rate is at an all-time high, especially in the Christian community.

Fear is also like a magnet; it draws to you exactly what you fear. Although you don't want these things to happen, you give power to them because they become your area of focus. Whatever you focus on, you give power to. Fear will cause you to put up walls, give up on love, and stay on an emotional roller coaster of toxic relationships. Our life is the manifestation of our words produced by our thoughts and influenced by our circle. Your words don't know that you're just playing or just kidding. They don't know that you really don't want these things to happen in your life. This is why you have to conquer those fears.

The only way fear can be defeated is by facing it with truth. The truth is you will get married. The truth is your husband is looking for you. The truth is you are beautiful.

Write down your fears. Find a scripture that combats that fear. Whenever that fear is presented before you, speak truth.

Unbreak Your Heart

....

Love and happiness can't flow through a heart that's calloused.

SHAMIEKA DEAN, THE QUEEN OF RESTORATION

....

"I'm not bitter. I'm just keeping it real," I responded in defense of my character. "I forgave them, and I've moved on with my life." Not convinced of my answer, I heard Lisa say, "Shamieka, you have bitterness in your heart. You have to deal with that."

Lisa is a very good friend of mine. At the time she told me this, I wasn't trying to hear her because I denied the very idea of being bitter. How could I be bitter when I had forgiven the ones who had hurt me and I had moved on with my life? This just wasn't possible. Being bitter was something I never wanted to be, especially since I saw so many bitter women in my lifetime, and it was very unattractive to me. I refused to believe I had become the very thing I despised. For the next few weeks, the word *bitter* kept popping up. I would hear it on a broadcast, see it on social media, or end up talking to someone about it. If you know anything about repetition, it's one of the ways God speaks to us which I will discuss later in the book. When something keeps popping up over and over, God is trying to get your attention. Due to the repetition of the word *bitter,* I decided to give some thought to the fact that I just might have been bitter.

I spoke to God in disbelief. "God, I don't think I'm bitter. I'm just wise and cautious. I keep it real like many others are afraid to. Is that bitter?" God didn't reply the way I thought, but He began to show me some of the characteristics of being bitter—and I was bitter. My bitterness had been masqueraded by justification. I called bitterness everything except for what it really was. The reason my bitterness was masqueraded for so long is because I thought bitterness came in through bad relationships with men. It never dawned on me that bitterness could enter with any heartache you experience. Broken mothers raise broken daughters, implanting the root of bitterness along the way. This is exactly what happened to me. My mother is a woman who I would describe as strong yet broken. Even to this day, I can look into her eyes and see the childhood tragedies of rape, rejection, and abuse that she never healed from. I can see her struggle to give a love to me she's never experienced. Her fragile heart that longs for love is overpowered by the fear of letting others get close to her. My bitterness came in through my relationship with my mother. I had developed a deeply-rooted bitterness in my heart toward my mother that I completely dismissed.

Growing up, I felt rejected by my mother. I didn't get the love from her the way that I needed it. There was an obvious difference in the way she treated me versus the way she treated my siblings. Out of all of her children who either lived in, or lives in one of her rental properties, I'm the only one who had to pay her rent whether I had a job or not. She furnished all of their homes for free and still provides for them now. I had to pay her for the furniture I got from her. Even to this very day, I'm the only one she doesn't do anything for. I do not look forward to birthday gifts or Christmas presents from her like my other siblings do because I'm the only one who doesn't get them. I will never forget the look in my mother's eyes when she found out I was pregnant at fifteen. The look of great disappointment filled her eyes. I tried everything to remove that look from her eyes. I wanted my mother's love and acceptance so badly that I became an overachiever. I always went the extra mile just to get my mother to say that she was proud of me.

Although I gave birth to my daughter as a sophomore in high school, I graduated from high school on-time with honors.

I received academic scholarships and went on to graduate magna cum laude from college. I even furthered my education by obtaining my Master of Science in Information Technology. I'll never forget how crushed I was when I told my mother I wanted to go to college. I didn't get the congratulations you hear from most parents. I wasn't embraced with a hug or a smile. I was made to feel as if I thought I would be better than her because I had a college degree. My mom hated all of my exes, so when I got married to the one she did like, I thought she would be proud of me, finally. Shockingly, she was completely against it. This confused me because she was the one who suggested we get married. It seemed no matter what I did, it wasn't enough for my mother.

I wasn't sure if I could ever do enough to receive the type of love I needed from her, but I was certain that I had to get rid of the bitterness in my heart. In order for me to overcome this bitterness, I had to get to the root of it by revisiting that pain that got me here. God took me to the exact moment that bitterness found its way into my heart. It was the moment I was raped by the fourteen year old. As a ten-year-old child confused, frightened, and traumatized, I waited for my rescuer. I waited to be comforted by the one I thought would be able to make all things better. In that moment where I had lost my voice, my identity and my worth, my mother walked into the room with anger pouring through her veins. She did not embrace me. She did not comfort me or tell me that everything was going to be okay. She blamed me for the action, punished me for it, and left me to heal on my own. In retrospect, I know that it is because of her own brokenness, but back then, I was just a confused little girl who had lost a very precious part of her.

The bitterness was implanted there but was compounded over the years through the constant rejection. It was buried deeply within my heart when I received a call from my mother who was crying hysterically, her speaking was barely audible. She was sitting in the doctor's office after getting the news that her lung cancer had returned and metastasized to her brain. I told her to calm down, that I would be there as soon as I could. After the call ended, I packed my bags and drove four and a half hours to stay with her for a week and a half to be able to transport her to her appointments so that my other siblings wouldn't have to miss work. I had the liberty to do this as an online entrepreneur—my job went wherever I went. This wasn't a big deal because I had done it during her first diagnosis. After the first treatment, the doctor came into the room to let us know the possible side effects of the cancerous tumor on her brain, one of them being possible memory loss. I called a meeting so that my mom could let us know what she wanted done in the event her memory failed her completely. This would prevent any issues among us as siblings because we would already know what to do. She went down the line of all of the things and willed everyone something, including all of her grandchildren, except for me. When she did this, something in my heart broke, not because I wanted anything from her, but it was in that moment I felt like I truly meant nothing to my mother.

My siblings thought maybe she had made a mistake, so they mentioned that she had left me out, but she did not change it. She told them if something was left over from the monthly payment of one of the rental properties, they could give me some of that. I sat there numb as every ounce of hope of being loved by my mother the way she loved my siblings was snatched away by her thoughtless words and nonchalant attitude. I called my husband to tell him what happened and he was in shock. "I knew your mom always treated you differently, but this one is even hard for me to believe," he offered in disbelief. As I left heading back home, I sobbed like a baby the entire four and a half hours. I knew I was still hurting from the things she had done during my childhood as well as my adulthood, but this incident was when the root of bitterness had taken place. I shut my heart off toward my mom. When it came to her, I wouldn't allow myself to feel anything. I made the decision to honor her and be there when she needed me financially or for support during her healing process, but my hopes of ever having a relationship with her were over. I had convinced myself that I didn't need or want it. I still didn't believe that I was bitter toward her and just believed I was dealing with her from a distance.

As God had me to reflect on my actions that revealed bitterness, I had a hard time finding happiness no matter how much success I was experiencing in life. I was looking for fault in almost everyone I connected with. I was trying to find something that would let me know other people weren't as happy as they appeared to be. I immediately found the negative in every situation. When it came to my mother directly, I found that I was very short with my mother. Almost every time I heard her name, my emotions would change to sadness or anger. When I had to have a conversation with her, I literally had to pray before picking up the phone. I experienced no joy when I talked to her. I contacted her to check on her because it was the right thing to do. I eventually humbled myself and was able to grasp that I was indeed bitter toward my mom.

Now it's your turn. Are you bitter or just keeping it real? Some of the symptoms of bitterness are the following:

- You can't find happiness in life no matter how good things are going.
- The majority of your conversations are negative or harsh. You are quick to find the negative even in positive situations. You do not believe that anyone is genuinely happy and find joy in the downfall of others.
- You look for fault in someone's happy relationship.
- You believe all have bad intentions.
- You have major trust issues with everyone.
- You're angry more than you're happy and don't believe you can ever be happy.
- You're revengeful and struggle deeply with forgiving those who hurt you. You desire to see those who hurt you hurting.

Overcoming bitterness is possible, but not without first admitting it. You can't go into an AA meeting saying that you don't have a drinking problem and expect to be delivered from alcoholism. If you want to heal, you have to be real and accept that bitterness is in your heart. My problem with admitting I had a problem was that it made me feel weak and vulnerable. This is the problem for most who deal with bitterness, but acknowledging the problem doesn't mean you're going to stay there. It is necessary for you to be healed from it. Admitting means you're strong enough to take responsibility for your life and do what you need to do to get out of that place of brokenness.

You take responsibility by choosing to forgive those who have hurt you. Next, give up your desire to seek revenge on the people who have hurt you because hurting them won't help you. Then, start celebrating the happiness of others. Whenever you begin to celebrate the happiness of others, you're sowing seeds into your own life, and you'll reap the same happiness you're sowing into the lives of others. Finally, bitterness is overcome by love, the love of God. The love of God can permeate through a heart that has been made calloused by pain, giving you the ability to receive and reciprocate love. Ezekiel 36:26 reads, "I will give you a new heart and put a new spirit in you; I will remove from you your heart of stone and give you a heart of flesh." A heart of love will help you to walk a mile in that person's shoes. It wasn't until I took responsibility for my bitterness, and stopped looking at the situation as a victim that I understood my mother's actions. She was a broken woman who had also become bitter. My mother went through just as much, if not more pain than I did growing up. Unlike myself, she didn't heal. She wasn't able to love me the way I needed her to because love is something she never knew. My bitterness turned into compassion once I put myself in her shoes. My compassion turned into prayers. The prayers led to my healing, and the restoration process began in our relationship.

Prepare

*I*t's one thing to pray for a husband but another thing to be prepared for one. I prayed for my husband and got him, but wasn't prepared for what I was praying for, so it went crumbling right before my eyes. Preparation for marriage goes beyond the beauty of your wedding and honeymoon. It's more than changing your last name, cleaning the home, and having sex with the same person for the rest of your life. In *Positioning Yourself to be a Wife*, the next step is to prepare for the man and marriage you're praying for. This preparation is to equip you mentally, emotionally, and spiritually.

How to Attract the Man You're Praying for

The right man for you will love you in your brokenness. He can help you through your healing process, BUT it's not his job to repair the damage caused by someone else. You can't allow yourself to remain broken with the mentality that "They just have to deal with someone like me." In attracting the man you're praying for this will not be by happenstance. You have to be intentional about your healing. Take full responsibility for going through the process to be healed from the pain others have caused you. If you aren't being intentional about your healing, your brokenness can cause you to break the one that God has sent you.

Think Again

The first thing to tackle is the way you think. Every action and word starts with a thought and whatever captures your mind, captures you. To conquer your thought-life, you have to be purposeful. If you want to know why you are thinking a certain way, think about what you are thinking about. In other words, if you are thinking about something sad, you'll feel sad and act accordingly. If you are feeling happy, odds are you are thinking about something happy. You have the power to change your thoughts. And how do you do that? You change a thought with a thought. Right now, count from 1 to 10. Now, say your abc's. Can you do both of these at the same time? I'm sure the answer is no. You just changed your thought.

Although the brain processes information extremely fast, it can only do so one thought at a time. The key to changing a thought is to capture the thought at its onset and not allow it to linger. The sooner you catch it, the easier it is for you to disempower it. Although you cannot control which thoughts enter your mind, you do have the power to control how long it stays. Romans 12:2 says you are transformed by the renewing of your mind. It's the consistent capturing and changing of old, damaging, and inaccurate thoughts with new life-giving ones. Those thoughts should line up with where you want to go. When you change your thoughts, you change your language. When you change your language, you change your life. This is why you cannot allow your thoughts to be consumed with the negative experiences of the past or negative views of men. If you do, you'll begin to speak that which carries me into the next topic.

Speak What You Seek

Delete your vocabulary of any negative talk about men. If you say things like, "All men are dogs" or "Good men no longer exist," you're giving these statements power and speaking those things into existence. These are the outward results of inward trust issues and are not reality. There are plenty of good men out there praying for their wife just as hard as you're praying for your husband. But if you continue to say negative things, good men won't find you because that's not what a good man is looking for in a wife. This type of language will make a man feel as if he can never be good enough for you. You'll look beyond the good in him because you've conditioned your heart to believe the worst in him. One of the statements I used to say was, "I don't need a man." This statement will run a man off quicker than anything because a man was created to protect and provide. Just because you allow a man to help you carry the load doesn't mean you're not strong enough to carry it by yourself. Although you do not need a man to validate or complete you, a man has to be able to fulfill a need in your life. This is his God-given assignment and makeup. If you strip him of that opportunity by telling him you don't need him, he will go where he feels needed. I used to say that to my husband all of the time, until I realized what I was doing. The reality is there are certain things I don't like to do or want to do. So, I gladly allow my husband to be the man he was created to be, serve the need he was created to, and I am his biggest cheerleader while he does it. I'm there with my pom poms screaming, "You better go boy! Give me a P! Give me an A! Give me a R! Give me a N! Give me an E! Give me a L . Give me another L! What does that spell? Parnell! Woo hoo!"

Even if your past has consisted of toxic relationships, betrayal, and heartache, you have the power to speak those things that be not as though they were (Romans 4:17). Your future does not have to look like your past, but if you continue to speak of your past, you'll create a repeat of that in your future.

Close the Doors

Whenever you leave the door opened to your past, it will find it's way into your future. Unresolved matters of the heart need to be dealt with quickly, and you have to completely close the door to your past if you do not want it to destroy your future. Closing the doors to your past is about destroying ungodly soul ties. A soul tie is any type of spiritual bonding that can occur between two people who have entered into any kind of personal relationship. Any relationship that is dysfunctional, degrading, impure, or pulls you away from God, is an ungodly soul tie that needs to be broken. Soul ties can be good or bad. A bad soul tie is an ungodly soul tie. An ungodly soul tie is not only formed with someone you're in an intimate relationship with, it can also be between friends, siblings, or a parent and child.

How are Soul Ties Formed?

Most soul ties are formed through sexual intimacy. When you become tied to someone, you become joined to that person. One of the meanings of the word *joined* in Greek means "glued to." In other words, when you have sex with someone, you become glued to them. Whenever you pull apart something that has been glued together, there is always damage to one or both parts, making it very painful. Sometimes when there is a separation of something glued together, a portion of one of the parts may remain attached even when the two parts have separated because you've now become one with them. This is why the heartache is so intense when you end a relationship with someone no matter if you're married to them or not.

How Do You Know if You are Tied to Someone?

If you haven't forgiven them, you're still tied to them. Unforgiveness will keep you tied to them more than anything else. You cannot break free emotionally, mentally, or spiritually from anything you're holding on to. Forgiveness of yourself is also important when breaking free from the soul tie. Remember, you cannot be free from your past if you're still living there.

Here are Some Other Ways to Recognize Soul Ties:
- You're still holding on to what they did.
- Your thoughts are consumed with them or what they did to you (good or bad).
- You're seeking validation from them by doing anything to please the person or to keep from being rejected by them.
- You have issues parting with things that remind you of them.
- You find ways to stay connected to them through family or friends, old hangout spots, or social media.

Things that Can Keep You Tied to Someone
Anything holding you captive to the memory of that relationship can keep you tied to them.

Refusing to cut off communication keeps the door open for reentry. When you're trying to break free from that relationship, you can't take any chances of possible reconnection.

- Gifts will keep you tied to them, especially if receiving gifts is your love language. It's not the gift in particular, but the emotional attachment that serves as a constant reminder of the good times you had in that relationship.

- Music is one of the most overlooked, yet most influential tools that keeps you tied to an old relationship. Think about how powerful music is. It is so powerful that young children listen to certain music and want to become drug dealers and murderers. The music makes them think it is a way to be accepted. Strippers turn into seductive machines listening to certain music. Beyoncé said that her music makes her become a completely different person—she's Beyoncé in real life, but Sasha Fierce when she's on stage. Music feeds your mind, emotions, and spirit, so you cannot underestimate its influential and transformational power.

- Love songs or songs that remind you of sex are off limits. If you listen to R. Kelly's songs, "Honey Love" and "12 Play," you will end up rumbling in those sheets on a lonely night real quick or Rihanna's song, "Unfaithful" which is one of those emotional songs that make you want to fight or seek revenge.

- Romantic movies that remind you that you're alone. Movies that you may have watched together are not a good idea. It is all a ploy to capture your mind so that you will go backwards instead of moving forward. It's a trick of the enemy. If you are not intentional about moving forward, he will give you amnesia about all of the bad things you experienced. Before long, you'll begin to downplay the severity of what caused your relationship to end. You'll make excuses for giving it another try only to end up broken again.

- Frequenting places you used to hang out together. Limit the number of times at places you used to hang out together if you know these places will remind you of those good times and pull you back into that emotional head space. You want to distance yourself from those familiar places that will cause you to begin to desire what you used to have. Also, finding new places to spend time is exciting. Out with the old and in with the new.

- Mutual friends. Limit the time spent with any mutual friends you may have where he may pop up. You don't have to stop talking to mutual friends; however, you do want to make sure your friends know that the topic of your past relationship is off limits. Let them know you're not interested in them trying to set you back up together, so if your ex is going to be around, don't invite you. If you're aware that he may be around when you visit the mutual friend, don't put yourself in that predicament. Leave or decline offers to attend events he's also likely to attend until you're completely set free from that relationship.

How to Break a Soul Tie

The process of breaking a soul tie is broken down into five steps: reveal, repent, renounce, remove, and restore.

1. **REVEAL** by asking God to show you any person you're ungodly tied to. Sometimes you may not understand that

there is a soul tie or that it is ungodly. Acknowledge that the soul tie is there so that you can start the breaking process. Acknowledgement has to take place because God can't heal what you refuse to reveal.

2. **REPENT,** if necessary, to restore your relationship with God. You have to be in right standing in your relationship with God so that you'll trust Him enough to let Him take you through this healing process.

3. **RENOUNCE** means to refuse to live by; to reject; to declare that you will no longer engage in or support. You are making a declaration to detach yourself from that ungodly soul tie and any vows you've made with that person or relationship.

    Side note: The renunciation has to be done verbally, breaking every vow you've made with that person or have spoken over your life about that person such as, "I'll always be with you," or "No one can make me feel like you do." When you made these statements, you made vows to that person further tying yourself to them. When you're in love, you're in love with the person you assume you'll spend the rest of your life with, and saying things like this is making a verbal contract. In the court of law, verbal contracts are just as binding as a written contract, and it is the same way in the spiritual realm.

Use this Declaration to Renounce the Soul Tie

I renounce all covenants, pacts, promises, curses and every other work of darkness in my life that entered through ungodly soul ties. Release me the yoke of bondage, loose the bands of wickedness, and destroy every ungodly soul tie I've formed knowingly or unknowingly. Give me the wisdom and strength to remain free from ungodly soul ties. Let all future relationships be divinely connected by You. I plead the blood of Jesus between me and them, and I declare that the ungodly connections shall not be reconnected. Destroy the very root that caused me to develop the ungodly soul ties. In Jesus' name, Amen.

4. **REMOVE** yourself from people, places, and things that can keep you tied to this person. Cut off all communication unless the kids are involved. If kids are involved, make it clear that the only thing you will discuss are things pertaining to the children. Be firm and consistent in your no. Say what you mean, and mean what you say. Don't allow a temporary moment of being by yourself cause you to reopen the door to that soul tie.

Have a Waiting to Exhale Moment

Waiting to Exhale is one of my all-time favorite movies with one of my favorite actresses, Angela Bassett. The movie is based on Terry McMillan's novel about four women and their relationships with men. Angela Bassett played Bernadine Davis whose husband, after eleven years of marriage, decided to leave her for his secretary. As with any other woman, Bernadine went through a series of emotions. She went through sadness, anger, depression and then there was rage. In her moment of rage, she went into their beautiful home, walked into their walk-in closet, snatched down his clothing (along with some other things), took them outside and put them into his white Mercedes. Bernadine backed the car away from the house, poured gasoline all over the car, and lit her cigarette with a match.

She then took a few puffs of her cigarette, dropped the match into the car, and watched it burn for a few seconds before flicking her cigarette into the fire and walking off with strength. The Mercedes burned along with all of his things. Now, I'm not telling you to set a car on fire. I wanted to highlight the liberation she felt when she had her *Waiting to Exhale* moment. As she walked away from that car, you could see the confidence and strength she gained with every step. She got rid of the things that reminded her of him and their relationship. This is exactly what you need to do. Get rid of all gifts, music, or things that are keeping you emotionally connected to that relationship. This includes those photos on social media platforms. Don't underestimate the sentimental value of things that can keep you tied to that toxic relationship. It is imperative that you do what is necessary to break free and stay free.

5. **RESTORE.** Now that you've taken the steps above, your identity needs to be restored. When your soul is tied to someone, you've also taken on their identity since you become one with the person. Use this prayer to restore your identity and relationship with God:

Father God, in the name of Jesus Christ, thank you for your grace, love, and mercy toward me. Forgive me. Help me to forgive myself and those who hurt me. Restore my identity in You. Restore my relationship with You. Make me whole in every area of my life. Where I'm broken, heal me. Where I'm torn down, build me up. Where I'm weak, make me strong. Restore my heart, mind, and emotions. Show me who I am in You. Help me to believe and accept who You say I am. Help me to be who You've called me to be boldly and unapologetically. Help me to stand firm in my identity, so that I will never settle for less than Your best for me. In Jesus' name, Amen.

Build Confidence

Growing up, I always had struggles with my confidence. But there was one particular incident that destroyed all of my confidence. I experienced the type of betrayal that no girl ever wants to experience, especially by her high school sweetheart. High school years are supposed to be fun and memorable, but unfortunately, I didn't have that story.

I waited by the boys locker room for my star player to come out. I greeted him with a hug and kissed him on the cheek to congratulate him on his win. I told him about a party at a local club that I wanted us to go to, and he agreed to meet me at the club after he changed out of his sweaty basketball uniform. Just as I was walking away, my best friend approached me wanting to know what my star player and I were doing after the game. I gave her the details and she let me know that she would be attending the party too. I walked back across the gym to get my cousin, who was accompanying me, and headed out to the club. We drove out to the club. You could hear the song, "Back that Thang Up" by Juvenile playing before you entered the door. We walked in, saw a few of our friends standing against the wall, and joined them. We stood there listening to songs and having conversations over the music. It was always a good time when we got together. Drinks, dancing, and laughter—the night was going fairly well. Suddenly, a song came on that shifted my entire mood. I couldn't really explain why I felt that way about this song I had listened to so many times. The song pierced my heart for some reason. The vocalist, Kelly Price sang so beautifully (as she always does), as her lyrics detailed how she put her trust in her best friend, only for her friend to lie, plot, and sleep with her man.

With each lyric my heart sank lower and lower. What was happening to me? Why this song, this feeling on this night? Suddenly, I felt a certain urgency to leave. After all, I had been waiting on my best friend and star player for over an hour to meet me at the club. "Where is he?" Worried and confused, I decided to drive to his house to see if he was there. My cousin decided to tag along with me.

Before I went to his house, I decided to drive by his cousin's house to see if maybe he stopped by there on the way. His younger cousin was riding up on a bike and asked me if I was looking for my star player. "He left in the white car with those girls." The white car was a Buick driven by a mutual friend of ours. She and my best friend always rode together. I thought they were somewhere smoking since they all used to smoke together. I tried to dismiss the nagging feeling in my stomach, but the next seven minutes to his house would turn out to be one of the most gut-wrenching experiences a woman could ever experience in her life. Everything in me was telling me that my heart was on it's way to being shattered, yet I continued to give him the benefit of a doubt. There was no way he would have me waiting for him while he was with another woman. But when I pulled up to his parents' house, I saw his truck parked in its normal spot. I said to myself, "Maybe he stopped by to pick something up from the house."

I creeped up those same four steps that were oh so familiar to me during our times together and eased the screen door open to prevent making noise that would awaken his parents. I walked into the bedroom, gently closed the bedroom door behind me, and quickly flipped on the light long enough to see if he was there and to make sure nothing was going to cause me to trip and fall. There he was. "My baby was tired, so he came home and fell asleep. I'm tripping for nothing." I said to myself.

I called his name as I sat on the bed next to him, but I heard a voice of panic. "What's wrong with you?" I asked as I jumped up to flip the light back on. I knew something wasn't right at this point. I looked at the floor and there were these cute little purple, satin panties. At this point, I'm thinking, *Either he's an undercover woman, or I just walked in on one of the most devastating moments of my life.* The pain I felt when I saw another set of legs in the bed made me almost wish the first assumption were true. "I just want to know who she is and what is it about her that would make you want to break my heart like this?" I demanded. When I pulled the cover back, I couldn't believe my eyes. I was in disbelief. The heartache of utter betrayal went through my heart, feeling like someone had snatched my heart out of my chest and ripped it to shreds right before my eyes. Never in a million years would I have ever thought I would uncover the face and body of my best friend. No one could've made me believe that this would happen to me. I was loyal to my friends. My friends were considered family. If you messed with them, you messed with me. What could I have ever done to deserve this?

I was in such a state of shock that I turned and walked out. I was so numb at that point not knowing whether to cry, fight, run, or hide. I just couldn't fathom what I had just seen with my own eyes. *Was I dreaming? Somebody please wake me up from this nightmare. Oh, how I wish somebody would pinch me right now and tell me that it's all in my head.* With every step I took, the ache of my heart increased and the pain became almost unbearable. At one point, I felt like my oxygen had just been cut off. I made it outside trying to register what I had just witnessed and my cousin, who was waiting in the car, prompted me with multiple questions that brought clarity to my thoughts and triggered me to go back in the house.

I walked back up to the house, snatched the screen door opened, and shoved open the bedroom door. He was sitting on the side of the bed, and she was sitting up in the bed with the comforter pulled up over her breast. He looked at me and started walking toward me because he knew what time it was. "If you touch me, I'm going to give you what I'm going to give her," I warned. He threw his hands in the air and stepped back. In a flash, I was on top of her beating her for dear life. I'm not sure how long I was on top of her. I just remember his brother coming from what seemed like out of thin air and scooping me under my arms, pulling me off of her. When he picked me up, I kicked her head into the headboard. The news about the incident spread fast. It happened on a Friday night, but by Saturday my phone was blowing up with people wanting to know the details. Every time I told the story, it was like pressing rewind on a sad movie. I knew that when I got to school Monday, all eyes would be on me. I was prepared to deal with the questions, but what I wasn't prepared to deal with were the lies she had everyone else believing. I was painted to be the villain simply because my past track record was that of a fighter with jealousy issues. The ironic part is that I never had any fights with a girl over a man before this incident. Although I had a few arguments and bumps in the hallways, none of those were fights over a boy until him.

The biggest dagger in my heart was that he stood by her side through this. He even told me that he was upset at me because I fought her, making him look bad. What a slap in the face! The lies, the stares, and the shame sent me into a deep depression. For at least a week, I didn't comb my hair, and I didn't care what I had on. I was there physically, but mentally and emotionally I was still at his parents' house that night getting my heart ripped to pieces right before my eyes. The type of pain that I was feeling was so intense, that even describing it as just being hurt was an understatement. I couldn't put it in words. With all of the pain I had experienced, my heart still longed for what I knew wasn't good for me. My mind reverted to the rejected, fatherless little girl who needed to feel validated—the ten-year-old girl who was raped twice, needing to take her identity back. I needed to win him back, because I needed to prove that I was worth being loved.

A few weeks passed by and we slowly started back talking on the phone. Afraid to ask the question because if the answer had been yes, my heart wouldn't be able to take it, I asked him if he was still involved with her. He told me they stopped sleeping together. In the depth of my heart, I didn't really believe him. However, because that little girl inside needed validation, I shoved my feelings into my back pocket and allowed him back in. He entered my heart and then my body. There I was giving myself away to him once again. While putting my clothes back on after having sex with him, he told me that we had to keep it a secret. As if I hadn't gone through enough heartache in my moment of vulnerability, I thought, *Are you kidding me? Let me get this straight! You hurt me by sleeping with my best friend and now you want me to keep it a secret because you're worried about what people are going to think about you?*

The fact that he told me to keep us a secret made me feel lower than dirt, humiliated, and embarrassed. That was the end of this, so I thought. I refused to sleep with him anymore thinking no man would degrade me like this. I wish those statements were true, but they weren't. I had no confidence and clearly didn't love myself at this point because after a brief separation, eventually we started back sleeping together. Each time I felt even more humiliated. About a month and a half of our secret love affair, I was finally fed up. I needed a title if we were going to continue sleeping together. Initially, he said he had to think about it because he wasn't really ready for all of that, but a few days passed and he made it official. He called me his girlfriend. You would've thought I had won the lottery. Finally, I had the title which made me feel secure in my position. Being called his girlfriend made me feel special, loved, wanted, attractive, and appreciated. The one I loved with all of me, loved me too! I assumed that the cheating would stop for sure because we were now officially a couple. Everyone knew we were a couple at this point, but that didn't stop those women from pursuing him. And unfortunately, it didn't stop him from being captured either. There were so many women I eventually lost count.

My confidence took an even deeper dive because the constant cheating and ultimate betrayal made me feel as if something was wrong with me. I began to compare myself to all of the girls he slept with, some of them had prettier hair, some were lighter complexion, some came from a home with both parents, and none of them had a child. I found something better about each of these women that made me continue to reject myself. At this point in my life, I could've written a book on how not to be confident. He had damaged my self-esteem so much that even after we broke up, I continued to stare at the ground to avoid making eye contact with people because I felt just that ugly.

For years I wouldn't even look in the mirror due to my brokenness. I thought that my nose was huge because a boy in my class called me "big nose" one day. It took years to repair from this damage that caused me to attract other guys into my life that played on these insecurities. We date at our level of confidence, accepting certain behaviors when we do not feel like we deserve any better. This is why confidence is so important because you will settle for less than God's best if you lack confidence.

Confidence is commanding the room without uttering a word, letting your presence speak for you.
SHAMIEKA DEAN, THE QUEEN OF RESTORATION

Every woman needs to know who she is before she tries to be anything to anyone else. You should exude confidence. I surveyed a group of men asking the question, "What makes a woman attractive?" The results were startling. It was not her body, education, or social status. It was her confidence. Confidence is a lifestyle! You have to live it, breath it, be it. It is not about how you dress or the makeup you wear, but being who you are boldly and unapologetically. In *Positioning Yourself To Be a Wife*, confidence is important for two reasons. Confidence will attract the right man and keep you from settling for the wrong one. You do not want to look up ten years from now and say, "I settled." You want to be able to say, "I'm happily married."

No matter how put together you are on the outside, only true confidence will attract a real man. Insecurity will only attract a man who will play on those insecurities. You set the tone for how others will perceive you and treat you, so if you don't see your own beauty, worth, or value, others won't see it either. When you believe it, others will too. Confidence is developed. It is a process of finding your true identity in God, your beauty beyond your physical appearance, discovering your purpose, and living life the way God designed. Confidence can be damaged by incidents in your past—whether it is because of things that have happened to you or things you've done to make you feel bad about yourself. Most of the time, it's destroyed before you get the opportunity to build it. The root to lack of confidence is rejection. At some point in your life, someone may have made you feel like you weren't good enough. Rejection runs so deep because when you take responsibility for someone's inability to love you, it can become your reality. You begin to believe it was your fault that your parents or exes didn't want you. The quickest way to get over rejection is to understand that the rejection had nothing to do with you. It wasn't your fault they didn't see the value in you. Rejection, although painful, actually realigns you with your true purpose in life. If you didn't experience it, you wouldn't search for your worth the way that you do.

When you are rejected, it forces you to discover who you are on the outside of what people have said, what statistics have determined, and what the enemy tries to make you believe. The rejection may not feel good, but it's for your good. Anytime the root of something has been identified and destroyed, you have to replace it with the right things in your life. It's like changing to a lifestyle of healthier eating. You don't just stop eating. You eliminate the bad food, but you have to replace it with good food that is going to keep you healthy and strong. First things first, you must acknowledge that the lack of confidence exists, understanding that false confidence is not confidence at all. You can't overcome what you refuse to acknowledge. The most dangerous thing to do is to lie to yourself. It takes a strong woman to admit she needs help. In building confidence, I want to talk about the 3 C's: comparison, conversation, and circle.

COMPARISON. Comparing yourself to others must stop immediately. From this day forth, don't ever compare yourself to anyone else. There are people who you can admire or people who will inspire you. But there is never anyone you should want to be but YOU! Comparison kills confidence. Theodore Roosevelt said, "Comparison is the thief of joy." You'll never be happy with yourself or in your marriage if you're always comparing yourself to others. Comparison sends you on an endless journey of trying to compete with someone else. There will always be someone with a better shape, sense of fashion, house or car, but there is no one who is better than YOU. Never place your value in the hands of others by comparing your life to theirs.

CONVERSATION. What you say about yourself will always have more power than what anyone else says. Your words shape your world. There may be things you are not 100% satisfied with about yourself, but it does not decrease your value. Believe it or not, Beyonce' is not literally "flawless" because she is perfect. She is flawless because she has learned to accept herself completely. This multi-grammy winning, iconic superstar didn't find her worth in things, but she found her worth within. Beyonce' has admitted her own insecurities in the lyrics of her songs. She could scream loudly about the things she doesn't like about herself; however, she speaks what she believes in spite of the imperfections that others may see. Instead of verbalizing those negative things you are not 100% satisfied with, change what you can and ask God for the courage to accept the rest. Negative language never produces positive results because you will have what you say. If no one else ever tells you that you're beautiful, good enough, or valuable, you must do so. You must become your biggest cheerleader. Your conversation has to line up with who God says you are.

One of the reasons God delays marriage is because He wants you to know who you are first. The promises of God are Yay and Amen (2 Corinthians 1:20), so the only reason for postponing an answered prayer is when what you are praying for will destroy you, or you will destroy it. As a wife, you're a helpmeet. A part of your assignment as a wife is to help your husband meet his destiny. You cannot help him meet his destiny if you don't know your identity. KNOW who you are! When you know who you are, no one can take that away from you.

The danger of not knowing who you are puts you in position to become whatever someone says about you. When you don't know your identity, you'll search for it in relationships, only to end up lost if the relationship comes to an end. It is important to find your true identity so that you won't search for it in your marriage. Another important point is knowing that there is a distinct difference in who you are and what you do. When asked, "Who are you?" you're more than likely going to state your name, job description, position, or title. Those things do not define who you are. Your identity is not in things, a title, a position, or job description. Your name was given to you by your parents. The titles and job descriptions were given to you by your employer. So, who are you outside of the labels placed on you? Without any title, certain position or type of car, you still are who you are. You are beauty. You are influence. You are inspiration. You are royalty. You are strength. You are powerful.

Who were you before the rejection or heartache? Who were you before the world told you who you should be or couldn't be? Go get her, and love her. Then affirm her and be her. Affirmations, or words of empowerment and encouragement, are the truth of what God says about you. They remind and reinforce who you really are.

God affirmed you before He formed you. He said you are beautiful in Ecclesiastes 3:11. He said you are fearfully and wonderfully made in Psalm 139:14. He said you are good in Genesis 1:31. He said you are far more precious than rubies and gold in Proverbs 3:15 and that you are a masterpiece in Ephesians 2:10.

Make a list of affirmations to begin speaking over your life. Post them on sticky notes, write them on your bathroom mirror, and keep them visible as a reminder to speak daily. When you speak, only affirm your God-given identity over your life.

The Lord had said to Abram, "Go from your country, your people and your father's household to the land I will show you. I will make you into a great nation, and I will bless you; I will make your name great, and you will be a blessing. I will bless those who bless you, and whoever curses you I will curse; and all peoples on earth will be blessed through you."

GENESIS 12:1-3 (NIV)

I always wondered why God told Abram to leave everything he knew, or why he had to leave his father's house. I know it is mostly about trusting in God completely, which is ultimately a test of faith. But there was also a deeper reason for this separation. It was because of the power in your circle of influence. Abram's father, a credible source and very influential person in his life, worshipped idols. Abram's family was a constant temptation for him. Our familiar surroundings and those who heavily influenced our way of thinking can hinder us.

CIRCLE. You are the average of the people you spend the most time with, and these people you are connected to greatly influence your life. Millionaires begat millionaires. Bitter women begat bitter women. Happy marriages begat happy marriages. Broken marriages begat broken marriages. When I finally became a wife, I lost some people. Notice I did not say when I got married, I lost some people. I got married, but I still conducted myself like a single woman in many ways like going as I pleased without any regard to what my husband said or thought. Most of my friends were fatherless women raised by broken mothers and had bitter and negative views of men. Many of them had a survivor's mentality which consisted of protecting their hearts from being broken. At that time, this was my circle because of the things we had in common, and I was comfortable in the mindset and our way of living. One thing about a good man is that he does not want his woman around negative influences because it will impact his relationship.

When I became a wife, my way of thinking, speaking, and acting changed. I took responsibility for my marriage and was now mindful of the actions that would cause problems. My circle said I changed and they did not understand it, but where there is growth, there is change. You are not still wearing the same clothing or hairstyle you wore in elementary school, and you've outgrown things that are no longer in line with your destiny. Your circle in life should match your destiny. Ask yourself, "Are my friends happy in their relationships? Do my girlfriends speak negatively of men or their husbands? Can I learn how to have a healthy, happy marriage from my existing circle?" If the people you are hanging with do not have a healthy view of marriage, then you need to adjust accordingly. This does not mean you have to cut them off completely, but you have to exercise wisdom so that you will not be negatively impacted by it. The people who are unwilling to change will cut themselves off. Now listen to the language of your friends and family. Ask God to reveal to you those who are negatively impacting your life, and give you the strength to remove yourself from that circle. Also, ask Him to replace them with those who will help you see the results you're praying for.

Love Is

If you're like I was, your definition of love is the longing in your heart for their affection or missing them when they're not around; spending hours talking about nothing or enjoying each others' company; holding hands, lying in each other's arms or someone making your heart smile. This is exactly how I felt when I met my very first love at the age of fourteen. I just knew he was "the one" and that this was love. After enduring the rapes, I had a true disgust for men. I didn't want to think of them or look at them. Years went by with me never looking at a guy. Finally, one guy, who I met through a mutual friend, caught my attention because he was very persistent. He told me all of the things I ever wanted to hear including promising to comfort me, protect me, and never hurt me. It didn't take long before I was head-over-heels for him.

The road to happily ever after suddenly came to a halt as I stood holding my face in utter disbelief, trying to grasp the reality that the love of my life had just slapped me with as much force as possible. Trying to gather my thoughts, I was slapped again. I struggled to keep from falling to the floor, but then the blows of his fist came like a whirlwind. He beat me from the living room to the bedroom and the final destination was the bathroom. With each blow, I struggled to keep my balance until I could no longer. I fell to the floor. As I slowly got back to my feet, he kicked me in the stomach causing me to fall backwards into the bathtub. He then proceeded to stomp me repeatedly all over my body as I laid in the bathtub, begging and pleading for him to stop. His friends stood by laughing and watching. In my mind, I didn't know if I would make it out alive. I retreated into the mindset of the rejected little girl wanting my dad to be my knight in shining armor and save me.

With pain all over my body, not knowing when the blows would stop, I curled up in a knot as I prayed to God for it to stop. Finally, he stopped and pulled me up out of the bathtub to check my body for noticeable bruises. Paralyzed with fear, I stood there with thoughts running through my mind, wondering if I would walk out alive. Embarrassment filled my thoughts as his friends stood by without offering to help at all. Anger consumed me, but fear took first place. As he touched the knots in my head, I squealed and jumped. With a smirk on his face, he told me that he had to hit me in places where bruises weren't visible, wanting me to have little to no evidence against him if I decided to press charges.

I was appalled at the lack of emotion he had, wondering who this man was standing before me with little to no remorse for what he had just done. He then apologized, but threatened me not to tell anyone. He kissed me and said, "You know I love you. I won't ever hit you again. I can't live without you. If you ever leave me, I will kill you. Now come on in here and give me some." I was disgusted feeling like I had to vomit. He laid me on the bed and began kissing my neck. With each kiss I screamed on the inside as tears rolled down my face. As he proceeded to have sex with me, I felt violated. I felt like that ten-year-old girl again being held against my will and forced to give myself to this man who had just beat me for dear life.

It only got worse from there. He began controlling what I would wear, where I would go, and who I would talk to. I could only wear clothing that were too big and could not go anywhere unless he went with me. I was so afraid of him. He made me look at the ground when we were out together. If I looked at another man or spoke to another man, the beatings would come. I would get beat like clockwork. As if the physical abuse wasn't enough, the emotional abuse skyrocketed when I found out he was cheating with women in his circle of friendship. I struggled to hide it from my family, until I could no more.

One afternoon, we were leaving his house when he became upset about something I had said. He didn't hesitate to pick me up and slam me on the ground. He was on top of me punching me when my mother came around the corner. One of the neighbors had recognized me and informed my mother of what was going on. She threatened him and told him to stay away from me. My mother told me to never speak to him again, but I thought I was in love. I continued to sneak around with him until it was too late. I found out I was pregnant and knew this unborn child would save me from the beatings, or at least I thought it would. The abuse slowed down, but it became more intense. I made the decision to leave because I realized that it was no longer about me. I was now carrying an innocent child, and I finally mustered up the strength to tell him it was over. He did not take the news very well, and began to pop up everywhere I would be. I threatened to contact the police, but he was not moved by my threats.

I was leaving a family member's house one evening and out of the bushes he came. He picked me up and body slammed me on the ground. I laid on the ground taking blow after blow to my face. The next pain I felt was excruciating from him pouncing into my pregnant stomach with his knees. All I could think was, *Lord, please don't let my baby die.* I held my arms over my stomach to prevent as much damage as possible hearing him say, "If I can't have you, nobody can have you because I'm going to kill you and this baby." He began choking me to the point I couldn't breath. I was gasping for air, unable to scream. I closed my eyes believing this was the end for me and my unborn child.

With my eyes closed, I visualized the relationships of friends and family members who were also victims of abuse. Suddenly, I heard a voice that said, "Not you." I opened my eyes trying to figure out who said it. The words began to repeat in my ear, "Not you! Not you! Not you!" It was so strong I began saying aloud, "Not me! Not me! Not me!" Apparently the words scared him because out of nowhere, I found the strength to wrestle him off of me as I repeated those words, "Not me!" I looked him in the eyes and told him, "Not me. Not now! Not tomorrow! Not ever again! This is the last day you will put your hands on me." There was fear in his eyes that caused him to flee. That was the day I was no longer a victim! I had been set free from abuse! I can't say I immediately knew what love was at that point, but I certainly knew what love was not.

To know if he loves you, you have to have the right definition of love. To truly define love, it is defined by understanding who God is. God didn't just tell us He loved us, He showed it, which means love is an action. He did not have to love us, but He chose to, which means love is a choice. God made promises and covenants with us as an act of love, which means love is commitment. God gave up something so precious to Him, which means love is sacrifice. God takes care of us physically and financially, which means love is protection and provision. God never changes toward us, which means love is trust. God is not prideful, which means love is humility. God is patient and merciful toward us, which means love is longsuffering. God honors marriage, which means love is honorable. God covers a multitude of sin, which means love is graceful. Love is not pain. Love is not jealousy. Love is not control. Just like God, love does not hurt. Love heals!

Find You First

Growing up, I thought marriage was the thing that solidifies living a happy life. I remember planning out my wedding as young as a middle schooler. My friends were my bridesmaids, and I was going to marry my high school sweetheart (I don't think he knew I had a crush on him way back then). I used to doodle our names on paper, using his last name as my last name. In my senior yearbook, there was a section that asked you to put your future plans. My ultimate plan was to get married to a fine husband. This was the life, right? Wrong!

Marriage should not be your life's ultimate goal. You were created on purpose with a purpose. Finding your life's purpose before your husband finds you is so important because you don't want to get married only to lose sight of who you are. You'll be more of an asset to him when you find you first. If you need him to complete you, you're not ready to get married because you'll become consumed with him. The marriage will become your identity (or your husband your god) which is something God never intended. Many people have committed suicide because they felt they did not have a purpose to remain on Earth. They felt a void which gave them feelings of hopelessness.

Understanding your purpose is the foundation to a life of fulfillment. When you are fulfilled, you have peace, joy, security, and satisfaction. Knowing your purpose takes away the feeling of emptiness and uncertainty. It is like being excited to show up to work every day because you know why you are there and that you are needed for the success of something. Your purpose has been screaming at you your entire life; however, when you are not taught how to identify it, you'll go through life searching for what's already within. Purpose is not discovered; purpose is uncovered. It's uncovered by digging deep, challenging things you've been taught, and finding the true essence of the person staring back at you in the mirror. Most people miss their purpose because they are too busy trying to find it, failing to realize it is already in them. Finding your purpose is a journey of self-reflection and self-evaluation, which includes finding your truth and coming into agreement with what you were created to do. You have a unique set of skills, gifts, talents, and passion that are the sum of your purpose. The passion that burns inside of you, the things you do effortlessly, and the unique way you do what you do are the outward manifestation of the purpose inside of you.

Your purpose is always greater than you. The purpose for your creation is to meet the need of another. The experiences of rape, teen pregnancy, rejection, and divorce were all a part of my purpose to impact the lives of women across the nations. If I had not gone through my divorce, I would not have the insight and revelation to be able to write this book. This book will help meet your needs and millions of other women who need to know how to position themselves to be a wife. It will help those who need to know how to forgive, heal from past heartaches, and have a happy marriage. The pain I went through was nothing compared to the purpose birthed from it. The purpose was greater than me and anything I've gone through. The things you've gone through in your life have equipped you with the ability to help someone who is where you once were.

If you need help uncovering your purpose, join my 7-Day Purpose Clarity Breakthrough that I've used to help many other women just like you uncover their purpose in just seven days. Many have uncovered their purpose and turned it into profit. Join here www.shamiekadean.com/purpose

Believe that He's Looking for You

....

"Therefore I tell you, whatever you ask for in prayer,
believe that you have received it, and it will be yours."
MARK 11:24 (NIV)

....

Praying is not hard, but believing what you're praying for is
where the challenge comes in. When your track record consists
of broken relationships, and you live in a world where divorce
is at an all-time high, it seems crazy to believe that happy marriages exist. To be honest, it almost seemed as if marital bliss
is extinct. After so many failed relationships, I thought maybe
marriage wasn't for me. If someone mentioned marriage to me,
I would respond, "Marriage is not for me. Most of the people
getting married will end up divorced or getting cheated on
anyway." Deep down inside, I desired marriage. I simply didn't
have the courage to believe that anyone would marry me. As a
matter of fact, my ex told me that no man was going to marry
me because I was a single mother with two children. He told
me that all I would be was someone's baby mama. He was
correct, according to statistics, my history, and the examples
presented to me. When it came to marriage, I did not pray for
it because I did not believe that it was going to happen.

When you believe that you already have what you're praying for, your approach changes. You do not go in with an, "If it's your will" approach. You go in with a "Thank you in advance" approach. A lot of people use the "Lord, if it's your will" approach because they are unsure of God's will, and they do not have the faith to believe they will receive what they are praying for. When you know God's will, you pray with confidence and expectation. When you finish your prayer with God, you will be certain that you have what you just prayed for, not walking away wondering *if* God is going to do what you've asked Him. You do not have any doubt in your heart because you know His will and have delighted yourself in Him, so you are sure that He will give you the desires of your heart. You have to believe that your husband is looking for you. You have to believe that you will walk down the aisle and say, "I do" to your husband.

Smile

"You look so much better when you smile."
Kirk Franklin

A smile gives off a good vibe, making others feel welcomed and comfortable. Smiling is also contagious. Think about it. Would you want to approach someone who looks like they've been sucking on a lemon all day? Would you want to approach someone with a frown or who's giving you a death stare?

I was headed to my car when I heard a male voice say, "Smile! It can't be that bad." My face must have said, "Who do you think you're talking to" because he stepped back, threw his hands up and said, "I didn't mean any harm. I just wanted to put a smile on your face," he explained. "You look so much better when you smile. I hope I didn't scare you. I just hate to see such a beautiful woman not wearing their greatest accessory, their smile. Whoever it was that took away your smile ought to be ashamed of themselves." I was rendered speechless but aware that my demeanor was so unwelcoming.

In that moment, I realized I had the resting face. The face that says, "Stay away from me. I don't want to be bothered." The face that is all about business and doesn't have time to play. I got that kind of feedback often growing up, but I didn't think it was a problem. It doesn't help that I'm a very heavy thinker. I could be having a conversation with someone and thinking about something else, which would be written all over my face. This was very challenging for me, but it's about being intentional. This is something I practice today, especially when I'm out in public. I make it my business to be friendlier and greet others first. Practice makes perfect and the sooner you start practicing, the better, so start now. Make sure you're cautious of your facial expressions when you're out. Make sure your facial expression is approachable. Every day isn't necessarily a great day, but make the most of it.

How to Confidently Know If He's the One

I was scrolling through the television one afternoon and stopped on an episode of The Oprah Winfrey Show. This particular episode she was talking about a vision board. A vision board is made up of photos and quotes that basically gives a detailed visual of the things you desire to have or accomplish in life. A couple of days later, I found the scripture Habakkuk 2:3 that tells you to write the vision and make it plain. This was confirmation for me that what Oprah was talking about was also a biblical concept. I had always written down my thoughts, but I never really wrote a clear vision for my life (unless you count the section in my senior yearbook). However, I figured if this worked for things such as homes, cars, and careers why wouldn't it work for a husband. On this journey of seeking God and preparing for your husband, there will be counterfeits to come before the real thing, so you want to confidently know if he's the one God has for you. This is why it's important for you to first be clear on who you are, and then know what you desire in your husband.

Don't Complicate It

I wanted someone who would desire me for more than my body. I wanted someone who could love me past my physical appearance, and fall in love with my intellect as well as other great qualities I possessed.

On July 2, 2005 at approximately 11:20 p.m., standing in the stuffy night air with no sign of the wind blowing, I swatted what seemed like the millionth mosquito. The faint sound of "Lovers and Friends" by Lil Jon & the East Side Boyz featuring Usher played in the background as we waited in the usual long line to get in the club. Feeling exhausted after a day of barbecuing, fireworks, and stiff drinks, my cousins begged me to drive my car to the club so that there would be enough room for my out-of-town cousins to attend. Club Deville was the hottest club in the area back then. My first thought when I saw this club was *I am certainly going to hell for this.* There I stood looking at this red brick building with stained windows that greatly resembled a church.

My attitude was stank this night. In other words, I was rude, snippy, and my face was frowned up. I had the "Don't say anything to me or you will get cussed out" look all across my face. There I was standing in the middle of the dance floor with my pin curled ponytail, orange-fitted T-shirt and khaki capri pants; my favorite orange sandals with the cute four inch heel, and arms folded with the intentions of warding off any guy from even thinking about approaching me. Banging through the speakers was my anthem. You know the song that makes you forget all of your troubles as you toss your hands in the air and scurry to the dance floor? That song. It was "Bad Girl" by Usher. I swayed my hips from left to right and was lost in the moment. I didn't care about anyone or anything. In my mind, it was just me and Usher on the dance floor until we were interrupted by this tall, dark, and handsome guy neatly dressed in his navy blue blazer, perfectly creased tan khaki pants, icy white Air Force One's and a white collar shirt. "Let me dance with you!" he said. Completely turned off, I rudely replied, "No. I'm dancing by myself."

You might be asking, Why did you turn him away? He seemed like the picture perfect, storybook guy. Well, it may have appeared that way, but after years of dating players, I knew them from a mile away. I turned my back to him and he walked away. Seconds later, here comes this guy standing about 6'2", 185 pounds soaking wet with a red, black, and white Chicago Bulls throwback jersey, white shorts, red and white knee length Dr. Seuss socks walking toward me. In my mind I thought, *I know this guy with these ugly, long socks is not about to approach me. I am going to hurt his feelings if he does.* My facial expression must have shown what my mind was thinking, because his haste turned into a slow daunting step. I guess he figured he had come too far to turn around. There he was standing face to face with me, a brown-skinned brother with skin as smooth as a newborn. He held out the largest hand I had ever seen and said, "Excuse me, my name is Parnell. What's your name? Hesitantly I responded, I'm Shamieka. He smiled at me, Miss Shamieka, would you like to dance with me?" My mind said, "No! Absolutely not with those ugly, stupid-looking socks on." But my body completely defied me when my hand ended up in his. He pulled me close to him like he was giving me a church hug. (A church hug is where none of the personal body parts touch each other.)

We began to slow dance but rather than him leaning into me, he looked directly into my eyes with his puppy dog eyes. Somehow I must've gotten lost in his eyes because five songs later, I was still gazing into them. My cousin looking like a modern-day Rick Ross, walked up and rudely interrupted us. It was actually our routine. The routine was after the first song, my cousin would interrupt and ask for the dance to see if I really liked the guy, or if the guy was giving me trouble.

The smile on his face was of someone who had just found the woman of his dreams. "Thank you for the dance, beautiful," he said. He asked for my phone number. I gave it to him quickly. He let my hand go and walked off. I was shocked for several reasons. One, because I just turned down a handsome brother dressed like Denzel only to dance with one who had on Dr. Seuss socks. What was wrong with me? Maybe I was experiencing dizziness from the socks but something was certainly different. For the next hour, I stood there puzzled because my thoughts were filled with thoughts of this man whose hand I didn't want to let go of. I tried to snap myself back into reality, but I couldn't. The bright lights popped on as the deejay announced, "Last call for alcohol," which meant the doors were closing swiftly.

I never wanted to be the last one out of the club, so I rounded up my cousins and we headed to our vehicles. I was a little bothered by the fact that the guy with the socks didn't say anything else to me after "our moment" which was what I called our dance. I opened the door to my burgundy 2002 Ford Explorer, but before I got in, I took a glance to my left, and I spotted the socks coming toward me. My first thought was *This dude better not ask to come to my house.* He held my door open. "I just wanted you to know that I wouldn't want to disrespect you by calling you after the club, but I will call you tomorrow," he said. "It will be after I get out of church. I also have to push my grandmother to church in her wheelchair. She won't let anyone else push her and I can't make her miss church. Good night, gorgeous." My heart fluttered. I felt something different with this guy. The last statement he made is what gave me hope. This may sound crazy to you, but here is why the last statement he made stood out so much me. He mentioned church. Now, I know that doesn't mean he was an angel, but it did let me know that he believed in God as I prayed for. He also was the very first man to call me gorgeous. Most guys I dated always complimented me with words that referenced nothing more than my physical assets. The fact that he said he didn't want to disrespect me by calling me that time of morning let me know that he respected me as a woman and wasn't looking to just hook up with me for sex. By the way, he also had a low hair cut with waves that would make you seasick. I'll share more about how God exceeded my expectations with Parnell as the story continues to unfold.

I want to emphasize, "Make it plain." What do you want in a husband? Do you just want *a* husband? What if an ex-con who was convicted of murdering his previous wife approaches you and tells you that God said you're his wife? You didn't write the vision and make it plain. You just said, "I want a husband. I'm ready to get married." Think about those qualities you desire in a husband. What do you want him to look like? What do you want him to dress like? What kind of personality do you want him to have? What kind of prayer life do you want him to have? What kind of career would you like for him to have? This will help you to know for sure if it's God sending you your husband or the enemy sending you a counterfeit. Make sure your list doesn't scream perfection because there is only one perfect man who walked this earth, and His name is Jesus. Think in depth about the things you need that go beyond physical appearance or materialistic things. The vision should be realistic. One thing I know about God is that He always exceeds our expectations. He won't give you almost what you want because He is a God of completion.

Don't Follow Your Heart

Almost every romantic movie makes you believe that following your heart will lead you to your Happily Ever After. This was the belief for almost every little girl who watched romantic fairy tale stories as a child. If my heart wanted something, I blindly went for it. If the relationship had potential, I disregarded all reality. After all, you can't help who you fall in love with, right? You're supposed to follow your heart, right? This mentality left my heart wide open with several years of disappointment.

Before I met my star player, I was dating another guy the year prior through the beginning of my senior year. He was amazing in every way. He was from a good Christian two-parent household. In the past, most guys shunned me because their parents felt I was too much for them being that I was a mother already. This guy and his family were special. They accepted my child and me with open arms. He treated me so good. There wasn't anything I could ask for that he wouldn't do. But there was only one thing about him. Unbeknownst to me, he asked me to be his girlfriend during one of his breakups with his ex-girlfriend. I was oblivious to the fact that they had been dating, and apparently he thought that when the relationship ended with his ex, the sex didn't have to. About seven months into our relationship, I found out that he still had been involved with his ex-girlfriend the entire time.

He was the third man I fell for that broke my heart. I truly thought he was the perfect guy, but in retrospect, all of the signs were there. The type of guys he hung with. The times I would call and he would be gone late at night without a legitimate explanation. The times when his ex-girlfriend would pass us in the hallway and always have this smug look on her face. The time when my friends were telling me he was over her house and I refused to believe them. The times I went to her neighborhood and saw him over her house, but he said he was with his friend who was dating her sister. I ignored all of the signs because I wanted so badly to be in love. I prayed for the signs that God was showing me but instead of me being led by the Spirit, I was being led by my heart, chasing the fantasy of Happily Ever After.

It's important to follow the Holy Spirit and not your heart because your heart does not have a brain and cannot think rationally. The heart is emotionally charged, unable to discern what love really is. Following your emotions will lead you astray. You are to be led by the Holy Spirit, the third person of the Trinity. I like to call Him the mailman who delivers our packages (prayers and answers) back and forth between us and God. He is the one who gives us gut instincts in the pit of our stomach when something is right or wrong and leads and guides us into all truth.

"Howbeit when he, the Spirit of truth, is come, he will guide you into all truth: for he shall not speak of himself; but whatsoever he shall hear, that shall he speak: and he will shew you things to come."

JOHN 16:13 (KJV)

Our emotions can sometimes overtake us, causing us to ignore the red flags. Physical flaws can be covered up and charisma can flatter you. The truth can be fabricated by beautiful lies and bad habits can be hidden. Dangerous actions can be suppressed, but the Spirit doesn't lie. There are some things that the eyes cannot see, the heart will try to ignore, but the Spirit will always reveal. Submission to the Holy Spirit is important so that you will be able to try the spirit by the Spirit. You try the spirit within the person by the Holy Spirit (1 John 4:1). Basically, you're testing to see if the person is who they say they are, checking for counterfeits and manipulating spirits.

Always follow the Holy Spirit. Ask God to give you sensitivity to the Holy Spirit and the gift of discerning of spirits.

Follow His Voice

In order to know if it's God speaking to you, you need to know how He speaks to you. God speaks to us in many different ways. For example, God speaks to us through silence. Have you ever noticed that the words *listen* and *silent* have the same letters? This is because you have to be silent in order to listen. Although you can still hear someone while you're talking, listening is a form of discipline. The goal in listening is to understand, get clarity, and instruction. My prayer time with God pretty much went like this. I used to go into prayer, rattling off my want list. One of the reasons I didn't listen is because I really didn't expect to hear anything back. To be honest, it was quite spooky to me. I didn't know what His voice sounded like and didn't know how to differentiate between Him, myself, or the devil. I didn't think I was important enough for God to speak to me. God was busy taking care of the world so, surely He did not have time to stop and talk to me. If you really want to be sure it's God, you have to learn His voice and the way He speaks to you. You can only do this by spending time with Him.

Another reason is because I was too impatient not knowing how long it would take Him to speak to me. What if I had to wait an hour just for Him to respond to one inquiry? Who has time for all of that, right? So I would go in, ask for what I wanted, and leave. I was always in and out, and had done my deed for the day. I figured God would eventually get to my list and answer my prayers when He had time. Sounds familiar? I began to feel like I was going aimlessly through life, not knowing if I was following the right path or making the right decisions. It was in 2010 when a powerful elder came to our church. She was so profound in the word of God and could preach better than any woman I had ever met in my life. I was immediately drawn to her because of her wisdom and insight, and we became very good friends. She would tell me how she had a meeting place with God. Every morning, she would run to this hill in her neighborhood where she met God and talked with Him. As soon as she made it back from her run, she would go into her room to write in her notebook what God told her. I was intrigued by this and wanted to know how she always heard from God. I longed for the type of relationship she had with God.

I expressed to her how I would love to hear God speak to me the way He speaks to her, but He didn't. "He's speaking! Are you listening?" she asked. "You have to give Him time to respond." Up until that time, I rushed my prayers, hearing God very far and few in between. My normal routine was to tell Him what I wanted and leave, but I learned that God is more concerned about your relationship with Him than your prayer list. Think about how your boyfriend or husband would feel if every time you interacted with him, you did all of the talking and immediately left without waiting for a response. Imagine you meet a guy and say, "Hi, I'm Shamieka. I believe you're my husband because you are tall, dark, and handsome. You have to have a good job and excellent credit. You cannot have any children. God told me you're the one. Let's get married."

You do not give him the time to respond at all, but you marry him. He still hasn't said a word. You hope that he's really *the one*, but you don't take time to listen to him, so you really don't know. Now you're married to a complete stranger. You don't know what his voice sounds like, and you don't know his personality, but this is because you told him everything you wanted, never stopping to listen to anything he had to say. God speaks the loudest when we are silent because when we are silent, we are listening. We are not interrupting Him with our agenda, but actively listening for His. As I stated earlier, listening is a form of discipline. You will have to fight off the distractions to stay focused and oftentimes refocus your thoughts. If you're like me, when I get quiet I have a list of "to do's" that run through my mind. But you have to make your thoughts obey so you can hear from Him. A tool I use when this happens is to write down the "to do's" that pop up in my head. It tricks the mind into thinking I've taken care of that task. I also turn on worship music that exalts, worships, and praises God to get my mind focused. Once I'm in that place of oneness with Him, I just sit and listen for whatever He wants to tell me.

God speaks to us through people. There are three gifts of the Holy Spirit in which God uses people to speak to us. The word of knowledge is when God gives someone specific details about you or something that has happened in your life. It often deals with your past or present. When you hear a prophet call out someone's birthday, phone number, address, or tell them how many children they have, that is a word of knowledge. God gave me a word of knowledge about a young man I went to church with. I had never gotten to know the young man personally, but one day he asked me to pray for him. He was not specific in his prayer request, so I asked God to lead me in prayer for this young man. As I began to pray, God told me that the young man had been struggling with homosexuality that entered in through childhood molestation. I began praying against the stronghold of perversion. I prayed that God would heal him from the childhood tragedy and for his innocence and identity to be restored. He did not know that God had revealed that to me. But when I prayed against those things, he confided in me, confirming what God had already revealed. He told me that he had been molested by his uncle at age seven.

There was another incident where I was a part of a monologue collaboration. The coordinator had inboxed me on Facebook about being a part of the monologue. It sounded interesting, so I agreed and we met up for the rehearsal. After rehearsal, she asked me if I would close out the evening in prayer. I prayed and the power of God permeated throughout the room. I was so overtaken by the presence of God, I couldn't shake it. As I glanced around the room, the women were in tears. "I have to be obedient and speak what God is telling me right now," I said to the coordinator who encouraged me to do so. There was a lady sitting next to me who God showed me was a worship leader, but she had not been doing it because she was afraid she wasn't worthy, and He showed me another lady who had a back pain on her left side. Although I needed to operate in the gift of healing, God gave me a word of knowledge to let me know where the pain was located and what she needed healing for. I've also seen God use someone to speak a word of knowledge when a person is seeking to know God is real. He will give a trusted individual a word of knowledge about your life that only you and God would know. Most prophets are given words of knowledge about people because it builds trust between the prophet and the person receiving the prophecy. It helps them to let their guards down and receive what God has for them. It also helps the person to know if this prophet is truly sent from God.

The supernatural gift of wisdom is necessary to understand the things of God. We don't always exercise wisdom, especially when it comes to matters of the heart. There will be times when you will run across a good man and God will give you wisdom to not allow yourself to fall for this man, because although he may be a good man, he may be bad for you. Following the wisdom of God will save you the disappointment and heartache. There was a really good guy who was madly in love with me. He was a church-going guy, who came from a great family and loved kids, and he would do all that he could to win me over. We went out on a couple of dates, and he would even try to buy me things for holidays. But God kept telling me that although he was a good guy, he wasn't for me. Every time I would think about giving him a chance, something would intervene. I tried remaining friends with him, but he was persistent, always wanting to take it to the next level. After talking to him more, I found that he was extremely insecure and also suffered badly from depression. He also did not believe a woman is supposed to preach. If I had married him, I know I would not have been able to freely fulfill my God-given destiny. I would not be happy because you cannot satisfy another person's insecurities. If anything, the insecurities would have increased as God expanded my platform. The depression could have easily attached itself to me because I used to suffer with depression myself. To this very day, he has not changed in those areas, and we remain on two completely different paths spiritually. He's still a very good guy; he just would've been bad for me.

God also uses the gift of prophecy to speak to us. Prophecy is a prediction or foreknowledge that speaks to your future. It helps you to understand your God-given destiny. Prophecy also serves as encouragement and confirmation. Every person that releases a prophetic word is not a prophet, but God can use anyone to give you a prophetic word. Prophets operate on a higher level of consistency, and most often, speak of future events. True prophecy will connect with your God-given destiny, gifts, and desires. For example, at the beginning of the year, I asked God what was the prophetic word for this season. He told me, "This is the year that the unknown will become known. Those who have been serving behind the scenes are coming to the forefront. Doors will be opened speedily. It will be a domino effect. People you've never heard of will start popping up and their influence will grow rapidly." I released the word and it happened just as He said. People began inboxing me telling me about the doors God was opening for them. There were so many unknown people coming on the scene who were taking off. People being connected instantly with some of the greats. It began happening so fast. I almost couldn't believe it. All of the gifts mentioned are ways that God uses people to speak to us, but be sure to measure the words spoken to you by the word of God. Don't forfeit seeking God and depending solely on people because anyone can make an error.

God speaks to us through repetition. In 2008 my husband was stationed in Fort Campbell, Kentucky. He was active duty military at the time. This was his second duty station, but this was the first one where I would accompany him. It was new and it was scary because this would be the first time I would ever live in a city of this size. Before the official move, I traveled down on three different occasions to job hunt, visit schools, and take a look at apartments. As a mother, I had to make sure the neighborhood and schools were good for our children. Each time I drove to Clarksville, there would be a bad storm. The first time, it was a really bad rain storm and the second time, a tornado was going through the town. (I was actually driving into the tornado; it looked as if I was chasing it.) The third time I got ready to leave work, my coworker warned me to be careful, that a snowstorm was supposed to hit the town that afternoon. "It seems like every time you go down there, it's some kind of storm." he said. "It sure is." I replied. "Maybe God is trying to tell me something."

As I drove into the town, the roads were covered in snow. It was so bad I had to pull over to the closest gas station because I could barely see the road and the car was sliding everywhere. I asked God, "Why is there a storm every time I come down here?" He said, "Because you all are about to go through a storm. But just like you made it through each storm on your way here, you'll make it through this one too." The repetition made me seek Him because I knew it had to be more than a coincidence. When God wants to show you something, He will continue to put it before your face. Are there any repeated scriptures, songs, incidents that continue to happen in your life? If you see repetition, ask God what He's trying to show you. You do not have to be a seasoned Christian to hear from God. God will meet you where you are and as you grow in Him, the way He speaks to you will change. When my children were young, I spoke to them in a way they would understand. I spoke the "goo goo, ga ga" language when they were babies.

As they increased in maturity, they were able to understand more mature language, so the way I spoke to them adjusted. When I first surrendered my life to God, He spoke to me through songs. There was a point in time when He only spoke to me when I was in a certain room of my house or when I was on my way to work. As I grew in Him, I began to study His word, so He spoke to me through scriptures and revelatory knowledge. The more I grew, the more He elevated the way He spoke to me. Eventually, I could feel His presence and hear Him audibly. It was a process and each person's process of maturity in Christ is different. Don't compare your journey with anyone else's. Grow at your own pace. If you do not know how God speaks to you, ask Him to show you.

Just Ask

You may have thought you found "the one" after you checked off those things on your list and decided to go for it. After all, he had almost everything you asked God for. You soon find out that almost doesn't count. After you've misfired a couple of times, you can begin to question your own judgment. The one you've met this time exceeds your expectations, but you're still not 100% sure. You need a sign to be sure because you do not want to end up in heartbreak hotel again. God shows you the sign, but when you're still not completely convinced, ask for confirmation. One of the biggest mistakes you can make is to move in uncertainty. There is a way that seems right to us but unless we have confirmation from God, our own thinking can lead us into a path God never intended for us to go.

I had written the vision and made it plain. Parnell was more than I envisioned. The kids loved him. He loved God. The family loved him. He made me laugh. He was handsome, compassionate, and more. Everything in me was saying, "He's the one." He even told me that he knew I was the one the first time we met because in a club full of people, it seemed as if I was the only one in the room. He said he told God that if He gave him a chance with me, he would make me his wife. However, I just couldn't risk making a commitment until death do us part to a man God didn't tell me to marry. Especially since we had only known each other for a couple of months.

There is a man named Gideon in the Bible who God chose to rescue Israel. The assignment would take courage because it was a huge assignment. Gideon was paralyzed with fear. He was afraid that he would fail. Like myself, Gideon knew God was telling him to do this, but fear still gripped him. He needed encouragement. He needed confirmation. He needed to be certain that he heard God correctly. So, he asked God for a sign, which was to let the fleece he was going to lay on the ground to be wet and the ground dry when he woke up. God did exactly that. The next morning when Gideon woke up, the fleece was wet and the ground was dry. Gideon didn't just say, "God send me a sign." He was specific in the sign he wanted as well as the time in which he wanted it to happen. God wants you to hear Him clearly. He wants you to make the right choice and to know His voice. God's will for your life will never contradict His word. The man God has for you will line up with His word. If in doubt, wait it out, but be specific when asking for a sign and confirmation. Even when you think it's the right thing to do, consult with God for confirmation.

He Will Love God

"Beloved, let us love one another, for love is of God; and everyone who loves is born of God and knows God. He who does not love does not know God, for God is love. In this the love of God was manifested toward us, that God has sent His only begotten Son into the world, that we might live through Him. In this is love, not that we loved God, but that He loved us and sent His Son to be the propitiation for our sins. Beloved, if God so loved us, we also ought to love one another."

1 John 4:7-11 (NKJV)

The reason it is so important for him to first love God is because a man who does not love God cannot love you like Christ loves the church. A man who does not love God cannot love you because he does not know what love is apart from God. God is love. A man who loves God shows it in his actions. It is not just about him going to church. It is about him exhibiting that love in his actions not just toward you, but also toward others. One morning, we were headed to Parnell's mother's house. He made his mother a promise to do something for her before she left for work. As we turned on her street, there was a young man who looked to be about sixteen years old. The young man had shoes with holes in them, and a shirt that looked like it was too small. Parnell slowed the truck down, rolled the window down, and asked the young man where he was going. I had no idea what he was about to do. The young man let him know that he was on his way to school. It was the first day of school. Parnell asked him what size clothes and shoes he wore. He asked him if he liked throwback jerseys, which were in style at the time. Throwback jerseys were expensive jerseys that resemble the uniforms famous sports teams wore in the past. An authentic one ranged anywhere from three hundred dollars to thousands of dollars. Parnell collected those jerseys, so he had about thirty of them just stored away at his mother's house. He told the young man to wait for him to come out of the house. A few minutes later, he came out of the house with four jerseys that still had the price tag on them, and a practically brand new pair of Air Force Ones to give to the young man.

If you could've seen the happiness in that young man's eyes, your heart would've melted just as mine did.

It was this act of love that confirmed that the man I loved had the love of God in his heart. Only a man who loved God would do what Parnell had just done. He saw a man who needed clothing, and he clothed him (Luke 3:11 NIV). He didn't just give him old, raggedy stuff. He dressed the young man in some of his best. He sacrificed something that meant a lot and cost him a lot for someone in need. He gave it freely not expecting anything in return. This is the love God showed us when He gave His only begotten Son for us. God made a great sacrifice for us because of His love for us. He gave us His best.

How does he treat his mother? Is he a man of integrity? Is he compassionate? Is he kind to strangers? Does he help those in need? Does he sacrifice for others? Does he show commitment? Does he exhibit patience? If he loves God, you will see it in his everyday actions.

Same God

Do not be yoked together with unbelievers. For what do righteousness and wickedness have in common? Or what fellowship can light have with darkness (2 Corinthians 6:14 NIV). A yoke is a wooden bar that joins two oxen to each other and the burden they pull. An "unequally yoked" team has one stronger ox and one weaker, or one taller and one shorter. The weaker or shorter ox would walk more slowly than the taller, stronger one, causing the load to go around in circles. When oxen are unequally yoked, they cannot perform the task set before them. Instead of working together, they are at odds with one another. Unequally yoked is not the same as being on different levels spiritually. We all grow in Christ at different paces.

Unequally yoked causes you to be pulled in two completely different directions, being unable to accomplish the assignment of your marriage. Whichever force is strongest is the direction in which you'll end up going. Therefore, you cannot afford to be unequally yoked with an unbeliever. For example, being unequally yoked is when you believe Jesus Christ is the Son of God, your personal Lord and Savior, but he believes in Scientology, Buddhism, or Elijah Muhammad.

2 Corinthians 6:14 specifically says do not be unequally yoked with an unbeliever. Therefore, it does not mean you knowingly marry an unbeliever and try to save them by marrying them.

"For the unbelieving husband has been sanctified through his wife, and the unbelieving wife has been sanctified through her believing husband. Otherwise your children would be unclean, but as it is, they are holy." (1 Corinthians 7:14 NIV) This means if you are already married, you get saved first, but your spouse doesn't. Many spouses get married and one gives their life to God before the other one does. When you married him, you are no longer two flesh, but became one with him. He's now saved because of you.

He Will Value You

We live in a world that has devalued women. Desensitizing the true worth of a woman's body by flooding the television with nudity and rotating songs on the radio that consistently degrade women. Women are viewed as objects, virginity is made to be uncool, and sex is no longer meaningful or sacred. The world has really summed up a woman's value by her physical appearance and her vagina. Women who choose to value their body as God told us to are left to compete with thousands of women who have neglected to do so.

What you won't do the next one will. If I don't have sex with him, he will just cheat on me with someone who will. I love him. I don't want to lose him. We are going to get married one day, so I may as well do it. These were the thoughts that plagued my mind when I contemplated having sex as a single woman. I was taught that the way to a man's heart was in his bed and through his stomach. Basically, if you could cook him a good meal and give him good sex, you would have him for life. At that time I saw sex as my most valuable weapon, and used it to get what I wanted to keep him coming back. Even if he cheated with someone else, I knew if I kept giving him sex, he would always come back. My value wasn't in who I was, but how I used what I had. I sold myself short for many years because of this mentality. I gave away pieces of myself I could never get back because I didn't understand just how valuable I was. I was so afraid of losing them if I didn't have sex with them not realizing my value wasn't tied to who left, but to what was left. Giving them my body along with my heart was giving them all of me, so when they left I was empty.

"Your Value Doesn't Decrease Based On Someone's Inability to See Your Worth."

SHAMIEKA DEAN, THE QUEEN OF RESTORATION

When my marriage ended, I was in a very dark place. I felt like I was no one because I had no one and couldn't fathom being rejected once again by someone I loved. I began to reflect on my past mistakes that caused me to feel unworthy of ever being married again. I felt invaluable. I was now a single mother with three children who all had different fathers. According to statistics and society, I was not on the men's "most wanted list" when they were looking for a wife. I had to figure out who I was. Months after my divorce, I found myself sitting on the edge of my bed feeling lost. I couldn't wrap my mind around how my life was unfolding and who I was as a result of it. Truth is, I was still battling some of my own demons and secrets. In a nutshell, I felt so unworthy.

God said, "Your value doesn't decrease based on someone's inability to see your worth." This statement was a revelatory moment for me because I had invested so much into my marriage and prior relationships that when it came to an end, so did I. Who am I without him? Who was I before him? Who was I created to be? I had the title of a wife and mother, but who was I? These were some of the questions that ran through my mind. With this very same statement, I want to take this time to encourage you. Never accept responsibility for someone's inability to love you. Don't you dare give that type of power to someone else. It's not your fault they didn't know how to love you. Some people we love don't know how to love us back. Sometimes we fall in love prematurely not knowing who we are really falling in love with. There are also times when we learn backwards where we are often taught what love is NOT in order to teach us how to appreciate true love when we get it. Don't take the blame for their actions simply because you chose to give love a chance.

The rejection does not determine your value and your value is not determined by what others think of you. Your value is not determined by the mistakes you've made, but the choices you've made in life are a reflection of where you were mentally, spiritually, and emotionally at that time. Sometimes you make decisions in life out of heartache and pain. Sometimes you make decisions because it's all you know and some of those decisions can be shameful, causing you to devalue yourself. Some of those decisions can make you feel inadequate or unworthy of being someone's wife. If you were promiscuous in your past, you may feel like you have to settle for whatever you can get. If you were caught up in an adulterous affair, you may feel like you've ruined your chances of ever being in a healthy, happy, prosperous marriage.

All of those things are lies. Forgiving yourself is vital to being able to receive the love you want and live the life you deserve. You have to separate what you've done from who you are and believe that your identity is not tied to your mistakes or failures. Your worth is not determined by the times you've fallen, but by the times you've chosen to get back up. God forgives you instantly, so forgive yourself as quickly as He has. You are worthy of being loved. You are worthy of being a wife. No matter what mistakes you've made in the past, you are still valuable. Hold your head up, girl. You're simply amazing just the way you are. Your future husband is looking for you, so hold your head up so that you won't allow him to pass you by.

Many women today have a "dessert first" mentality. They are afraid to hold themselves to a higher standard out of fear of him leaving for someone else. They offer their dessert upfront in efforts to keep him, but there is a specific order in the delivery of food in a restaurant (woman). First, the appetizer (courtship). The appetizer is just a small taste of what this restaurant has to offer. The appetizer is to stimulate his appetite. Next, the entrée (marriage). He saw the value in the entrée and decided it was worth taking the next step to purchase the entrée. Last, the dessert (sex). The dessert is given after the entrée. If the dessert is offered upfront, it spoils their appetite for anything else.

Anytime you bypass the entrée, you're missing out on the value of all of the nutrients (skills, assets, values, worth) it possesses. You place the value on what's on your menu. Every person cannot afford your quality of food and will not see the value in it. It doesn't mean change your menu or allow them to determine the price for you. It means you allow them to go to another restaurant so that you can keep yourself open to the one who will see the value and is willing to purchase the entrée.

How to Deal With Celibacy

I wanted this book to be REAL. Since I haven't dealt with celibacy in many years, I've solicited the wisdom of my friend and founder of Finding Me Before I'm Found, Courtney Aiken. In the next section, you'll be taken through the steps on how to deal with celibacy from someone who is actually walking the walk.

You're on the perfect date with the perfect man. He's so perfect that he can hold a great conversation, make you laugh, and he's giving you five-star treatment you've never received from any other man. The night is coming to a close, and the vibe and connection is so strong, it becomes an attraction. He takes you home, walks you to your door, puts his arms around you to hug you, and your flesh is rising up because it's been months or maybe even years since you've been intimate with a man. You have two choices: 1. Invite him in your home, be intimate with him only for him to leave after the act is over causing you to wake up full of regret or 2. Thank him for a great night, send him on his way, and wake up the next morning without a guilty conscience. One of the toughest and most dangerous parts of the waiting process in becoming a wife is celibacy. When you love and have consistently had sex, not having sex can affect you in ways you've never imagined. However, you have to wonder if a moment of pleasure is worth missing out on a lifetime of happiness because you cannot control your hormones. As good as sex is, you must ask yourself if good sex is greater than having a good marriage. When I was a teenager, I asked my mother about sex. Her response? "Don't have sex or else you'll get pregnant." I waited around for her to say more but that's all she told me. Now, it was old school teaching, but wisdom as well.

As a single woman, you must be careful of who you become intimate with because you can wind up pregnant and carrying something that you aren't built or equipped to handle. When you lie down with someone, your bodies connect into each other, and you don't know what you are entering into. He may be carrying a big piece on the outside, but even bigger issues and drama internally. When tempted with sex, you must ask yourself if riding his big piece is worth receiving his big issues. It may feel like the greatest ride of your life, but that ride can turn into a rollercoaster, causing you to go through ups and downs, highs and lows. You can use all the protection in the world to prevent yourself from getting pregnant, but it won't protect you from the internal demons you risk receiving and suffering from for years because of a few moments of pleasure.

So many people think with the wrong "head" literally and figuratively. In other words, having sex with a man won't make him become the head of your household because he can get sex somewhere else. Good sex will bring a man around you, but it won't keep him around you. What happens when he gets bored because you keep doing the same things when you're intimate? Changing techniques and positions can only temporarily solve the issue, especially if he finds someone else who excites him.

You must feed his brain! In order to feed a man's brain, you must know your position and stand in it. When athletes try out for a team, they go through a tedious process to be chosen and once they make the team, they must work to get into the right position. You have to decide if all of the work you've done to get in position to be found by the right man is worth losing because of your flesh.

Before my daddy passed away, my parents were married for forty-five years, and they taught me that as long as I focused on God, family, and my education, then at the right time, God would send the right person. In fact, they got married straight out of college right before my mother began her master's program. I never dated anyone throughout high school or college. I didn't feel the need to because of what my parents instilled in me. I was very focused on graduating from college with honors and beginning my career in law. A few years after graduating, I met a guy who became my best friend. We were together every day, and he shared his heart with me in a manner that he had never shared with anyone he dated before, or even family members. I helped him reconnect with his father who wasn't a part of his life as a child and teenager, establish a closer relationship with his family members, and helped him build his businesses. As the years rolled by, we developed feelings for each other; however, he had a thorn in his side which was his daughter's mother. He wanted to give his daughter the life he never had, which was growing up in a household with both parents. Although they had an off and on relationship, he had feelings for me and I wound up losing my virginity to him. Even though I knew he would go back to his daughter's mother when she would call, I still put myself in a position where I let my feelings get the best of me instead of common sense. We were intimate with each other for a year, and it ended abruptly when I found out on social media that he had married his daughter's mother.

After losing my virginity to him, I beat myself up because I made a promise to God that I would wait for my husband and deep in my heart, I felt like he would choose me over her. Boy, was I mistaken! I also felt like I cheated on God and lost sight of the values my parents instilled in me. After the intimacy ended, I had to go through a process of purifying myself and getting adjusted to celibacy. I promised God that my next partner would be my husband, and three years later, I've remained faithful to that promise.

There's a reason why God created intimacy for marriage. It is a powerful and enjoyable experience that if used in the wrong manner can put people in compromising situations that are hard to be released from. The first few months of my celibacy journey were tough, but over time there were some things I did and learned that made the journey much easier. Here are some practical steps in dealing with celibacy.

Physical Steps:

1. No "house dates" or Netflix & Chill. Your home is your sanctuary and you must be careful who you allow inside because you don't know what they are bringing with them.

People carry spirits, and if you are dating someone who comes to your home and may secretly carry the spirit of lust, that spirit can affect your atmosphere and safe haven. It's best to date somewhere that isn't a few steps away from your bedroom so that you aren't tempted!

2. No late night dates or meet ups. Become disciplined and put yourself on a curfew. Late nights and hours are when you can easily become vulnerable, and you don't want your vulnerability to lead to intimacy with someone. Meet up during the day so that you have a clear mind and conscience and aren't so tired that you don't think straight, and wind up in someone else's sheets!

3. Turn off phone notifications. Let the "DO NOT DISTURB" and "BLOCK" features become your best friend! It is so important to block former mates' phone numbers and their ability to text, email, or message you on social media. When you've had a strong soul tie with someone, seeing their name, face, or hearing their voice can easily tempt you. Trust me, I've been there! It's best to block them before your blessings become blocked!

4. Change your television lineup. Cover your eyes! When you watch food commercials on television, you can become tempted to buy and try certain food items. Don't become tempted by watching shows or movies that have a lot of intimate scenes because it can trigger your desire. Watch

inspirational shows or comedies to keep you off the edge and in a happy place.

5. Eat sugar. Studies have shown that sugar helps to lower sexual libido. Try to add some sweets on those nights where you feel the strongest desire. From my personal experience, going to sleep with a heating pad after eating either of these items will help you fall asleep faster and remove the desire.

Spiritual Steps:

1. Speak to your flesh. Proverbs 18:21 tells us that "Death and life are in the power of the tongue: and they that love it shall eat the fruit thereof." As crazy as this may sound, if you lay hands on your private area and speak for the desire to go away, it will. It may not happen instantaneously, but the desire will be released! When you feel like the desire is taking over your body, speak to the flesh and your hormones will get under control.

2. Fasting and praying. When you fast and pray, you are able to hear from God in a different manner and receive clarity in areas you feel are unanswered. Cutting out certain foods from your diet gives your body the chance to release any toxins that may be in your system due to old soul ties. You must not have any residue of the past and be toxin-free so you can have a clear mind, be free, and remain celibate.

These steps weren't researched for the sake of this chapter, but were used in my personal journey and actually worked. When you truly make up in your mind that you want God's best for you, nothing, including some good sex, will get in the way of that. It was after I became celibate that God opened MAJOR doors for me. I was so caught up in pushing someone else to become all that he could be and forgot about me! Being intimate with the wrong person will cause your vision and focus to become cloudy, and your only desire will be to please that person, even if it means neglecting yourself.

God's best for you will not let you neglect yourself nor the anointing or calling on your life. Understand that in order to receive God's best, God must first make you better. Celibacy is a journey of self-discovery that will cause you to look at yourself in the mirror and deal with all insecurities, low self-esteem or lack of confidence, and overcome rejection. Know that you are worth the wait! Intimacy is a beautiful experience that God created to bring a husband and wife closer. When you are intimate with people, you don't know what it's bringing you closer to! Sleeping with the wrong person can bring you closer to destruction, depression, schizophrenia, or a number of things. Before moving on to the next chapter with Shamieka, make the decision in this very moment that you want to take your celibacy journey seriously, and get ready for what God has for you. This journey will not only make you a better woman, but bring you closer to God and His plan for your life!

Position

*N*ow that you've been purged and prepared, it's time to step into position. You want to make sure you do what is necessary to sustain your position because you don't want to end up like Queen Vashti. In *Positioning Yourself to be a Wife*, prevention is the best method to sustainability. In order to do this, you have to understand the dynamics of marriage, learn how to play your position to win, and do what it takes to stay out of divorce court.

Marriage Defined

Growing up, I fantasized about the Cinderella fairytale. I actually felt like Cinderella growing up—rejected and unappreciated—not being able to do anything to be accepted by her stepmother. I recall my mother telling me to clean the kitchen one day. Everything had to be spotless or she would make me clean it all over again. I went into my bedroom and put on one of my Sunday dresses. I grabbed the mop bucket, and filled it with dishwashing soap and water until bubbles were overflowing. I was on my hands and knees with a brush in one hand and a mop in the other one. I was saying, "Mop the floor Cinderella," basically reenacting a scene from the movie. I still had to clean the kitchen and Prince Charming never showed up. I went on to believe that I would have to kiss a frog until it turned into a prince.

The fantasies of marriage turn into nightmares for many because marriage has been so misunderstood. We are taught that you meet this guy, fall in love, and live happily ever after. Most women plan the immaculate weddings and extravagant honeymoons, only to end up married and miserable. I was prepared for the wedding, but not for marriage. When I was found by my husband, my initial thought was that I am complete. The goal of marriage is never to look for completion, or to be made whole because being made whole in an inside job. Your husband should complement you, enhance you, add value to you, but never complete you. When we finally said our "I do's" I was convinced that as long as we loved each other, everything would be perfectly fine. This ideology is a guaranteed setup for failure.

Although we love the benefit of being able to be fruitful and multiply, marriage is more than that. It takes more than love to sustain marriage. If love was all it took, we would've married the first person we loved who loved us back. I heard on a TV show called *Chasing Life,* that "The foundation of marriage is love, but the reality of marriage is commitment."

This rings so true. Marriage is a beautiful love story, but it is not a fairytale. Marriage is more than a ceremony where family and friends gather to hear you say, "I do" to the love of your life. Now, don't get me wrong. Marriage is also fun, exciting, exhilarating, and adventurous; however, these things do not just happen. These benefits are a result of being committed to the ups and downs that take place in your marriage. Marriage is the tangible representation of the love God has for the church and the order in the kingdom of God. You cannot be passive about the growth and sustainment of your marriage. In other words, it takes work. This is why there is such an attack on Christian marriages. The attack on marriage is an attack on the kingdom of God, the love of God, and the sacrifice of Jesus Christ. This is also why marriage is not to be taken lightly. Understanding just how important marriage is helps to take the vows more seriously.

"Wives, submit yourselves unto your own husbands, as unto the Lord. For the husband is the head of the wife, even as Christ is the head of the church: and he is the Saviour of the body. Therefore as the church is subject unto Christ, so let the wives be to their own husbands in everything. Husbands, love your wives, even as Christ also loved the church, and gave himself for it."

EPHESIANS 5:23-25 (KJV)

When I look at marriage in alignment with the kingdom of God, the husband is the head, the wife is the neck. The other body parts represent the children, ministries, and any other tasks God has assigned to your life. God created male and female, two completely different creatures with completely different functions, roles, and abilities. There are certain parts of a male's body that work in conjunction with the female's body. I know we live in a world where women have developed a superwoman mentality, and it is absolutely phenomenal that a woman can provide for herself. We are strong women. You have to be strong to carry a human being, and go through labor and delivery. If you did it like me, you went through the birthing process all-natural. We have strength that still raises my eyebrows. It is amazing that a woman can do almost anything a man can do, but God created man so she doesn't have to.

In our home, we have certain things that my husband does and certain things that I do. It is not so much gender-specific as it is the things we are just really good at. One of the things my husband does is lift all of the heavy stuff. I got upset with him one day because he wasn't moving as fast as I wanted him to. I needed some boxes moved, and I wanted him to move them when *I* wanted them moved. I was so frustrated with the ordeal, that I turned into superwoman and decided to move the boxes myself. He saw my struggle and came to take the load off of my hand. Only if you could've seen the struggle I was experiencing in that moment. Imagine Olive Oyl trying to carry Bluto. My legs began to turn into noodles, and I was sweating profusely.

The box was so big I was barely able to wrap my arms around it. I was a true damsel in distress in that moment, but I was too prideful to call and ask him for help.

Somehow he found his way downstairs, maybe from hearing my grunts, or maybe the Holy Spirit quickened him to come on down. The look on his face was one of pity as he grabbed the box and put it where I wanted it to go. "Is there anything else you need me to help you with?" he politely asked, but I was so stubborn I replied, "No." I didn't even thank him for saving me. Later on that night, I told him I was sorry, taking back the whole *I can do what you can do* attitude. I let him know how much I really needed him and appreciated what he does. I realized that as stubborn as I could be, I no longer desired to take over his position. It was not about the box. I am sure I could've gotten it eventually. I know we probably had a dolly around somewhere if I needed it. But it was more than that. It was the revelation that God created us to do different things. It is not a weakness for me to allow him to operate in the capacity that he was created to operate in.

The husband or CEO is the head of the marriage which means God has placed him in position of leadership within the home. As the CEO of any organization, he oversees the success of the entire organization. His role is very demanding, and he's responsible for the protection, provision, and direction to lead the organization to success. It is very stressful because the weight of the world is on his shoulders. In order for this to work, he has to have the right supporting role which is where the role of the wife comes in.

The wife, the COO of the organization, is responsible for carrying out the day-to-day tasks associated with the overall goal of the organization. She is the support of the head, the CEO, which is the foundation for the entire body. Right now, try to move your head without moving your neck. You cannot do so. This is because the neck is the true driving force in the marriage. The success of the head and the rest of the body is contingent upon the proper positioning of the neck. The slightest jolt in your position can cause major damage to the entire body like an injury as minor as whiplash can cause long-term damage to every organ in your body.

If you're anything like me, this may sound like control. Coming from the situations I've endured in the past, this was very difficult for me. I feared allowing someone to lead me because I had trust issues and didn't understand. Once I understood what it really was, I was able to let my guard down and get in the proper position. What I'm talking about is submission. If you have been betrayed, rejected, or abandoned, this word may be scary for you. This word is like a curse word or a slap in the face to a woman who has been made to feel helpless or vulnerable beyond her control.

Play Your Position To Win

"Girl, I refuse to let a man control me. I'm a grown woman. I do what I want to do, when I want to do it. If marriage means a man has to control me, I won't be married. That is why I make my own money, and own my house and vehicle. I need him to know he ain't running nothing. That's why I'm not moving in with a man; he will have to move in with me. That way if he starts trying to run something, he can hit the door. I don't need a man for nothing but one thing anyway, sex. I can take care of myself. I was doing it before and I can do it if he decides to leave."

This was my conversation when it came to submission, and I used to wear the "I don't need a man" badge of honor proudly. Because of my brokenness, wrong way of thinking, and history of broken relationships, I thought needing a man meant I was weak and needed him to complete me, or I wasn't good enough unless I had a man in my life. At the same time, I couldn't figure out why I was still single. This is the conversation of many women who've experienced any form of abuse or who simply do not understand what submission really is.

Submission has been given such a bad reputation. When I thought of submission, I thought I had to give up my identity or another opportunity for someone to take away my voice and power. I rebelled against the very idea of submission because I was determined not to allow another man to ever make me feel that vulnerable again. Submission is not slavery and does not take away from your worth or value. It doesn't mean you allow your husband to belittle you or degrade you. Submission is not to be used as a weapon to reward or punish your husband for bad behavior or reward him for good behavior. Submission is not about your husband at all, but it is all about you and your trust in God. When you submit to your husband as unto the Lord, you are telling God that you trust His plan over your pride. You're saying, "I trust You to lead my husband so that he can lead me. I trust You to provide him with the wisdom, knowledge, tenacity, and skills to love me as Christ loved the church." Submission is playing your position so that the whole team can win.

I wish I had known this a lot sooner. It would've saved me a lot of heartache. Refusing to submit can cost you your position just like it did me and Queen Vashti. In the book of Esther 1 and 2, Queen Vashti, a beautiful, modern-day Halle Berry was married to King Xerxes the king of Persia. One night King Xerxes had a party at the house with the leaders of the community. In the other part of house, Queen Vashti was hosting a party for the women. After King Xerxes and the men of the community had been drinking, he called for Queen Vashti to come out wearing her royal crown to be seen by the men. Queen Vashti refused to submit to the direction of King Xerxes.

Queen Vashti had a problem with submission, which cost her her position. She didn't look beyond herself or understand the power of her position. She did not think about the affect she would have on her husband or the kingdom. She had the position she had been praying for, but she wasn't equipped to handle it. I was just like Queen Vashti in the beginning of my marriage. I did not understand the importance of my position or the influence it had on everyone and everything that was connected to me. I failed to realize that my marriage was bigger than me. The marriage God had blessed me with was not about me, but the mission He had for my marriage.

My refusal to submit cost me my position and my marriage ended in divorce.

Now that you have a better understanding of submission, it will make it easier for you. You will be more willing to submit to your husband not because he's perfect, but now you've learned the blessing in winning from your position! You understand how important your position is in your marriage and if you stay in position, your family has no choice but to prosper in everything you do.

You Are the Driving Force

Everyone wants to wear the crown, but few are prepared to handle the position. Queen Vashti's disobedience opened up the door to Queen Esther's favor. I had to become an Esther before God restored my position. I talked earlier about how the husband has to be staffed with the right people in the right position. This is because he has to have the right support for the success of the mission God has placed before him. The people he's responsible for leading have to be willing to submit to the vision God has entrusted him with, and he cannot lead a team that does not want to submit. He cannot function in his fullest capacity if his wife doesn't stay in position.

As a wife, you are your husband's helpmeet. Your position as his helpmeet will either help him meet his destiny or his destruction. Queen Vashti's position could not be left unfilled because of the assignment on King Xerxes' life. They had to quickly find another Queen to take her place. There were several virgins selected to go before the king and if they were chosen as Queen, they would be called back a second time. Queen Esther was the woman chosen to replace Queen Vashti.

What I like about the story is that the women were given the opportunity to take extra things other than what the king's eunuch Hegai had provided them with to make them more appealing to the king. Queen Esther did not take anything additional. I believe at this point, Esther was confident in who she was after going through the purification process. She had been healed of the old wounds from her past. She looked good inwardly and outwardly. Everything Queen Esther needed to take her position was already within her. She didn't have to take anything extra because the purification process prepared her to take her rightful position. Immediately, she obtained favor with the king and all who laid eyes on her. "A man who finds a wife, finds a good thing and obtains favor from the Lord" (Proverbs 18:22).

Queen Esther was different. Queen Esther showed that she was trustworthy and her ability to submit long before she took her position as queen. Remember, her cousin Mordecai raised her after her parents died. He was the male covering over her life prior to her becoming queen. Mordecai had given Esther instruction not to reveal her Jewish heritage to anyone, and she did not disobey Mordecai at any time. After Esther took her position as Queen, Mordecai's life ended up being threatened by an Amalekite named Haman. Haman had plotted to kill Mordecai and all of the Jews because Mordecai refused to bow down to him and reverence him. Mordecai went to Esther for help, wanting Esther to go talk to King Xerxes to save them. Esther proceeded to explain to Mordecai that it wasn't time for her to go before the king because he hadn't called for her. It was a deadly consequence back then to go before the king unless you had been called. Mordecai told Esther that she had to forget about herself because it was bigger than her. It was about the entire race of the Jews. Esther agreed. She said, "If she perishes, she perishes." She understood that her assignment was more than her title and her marriage to King Xerxes was bigger than her. She had to be in the position as Queen in order to accomplish the assignment on her life to save the Jews. Every God-ordained marriage has a mission and purpose far greater than the two people that said, "I do."

Queen Esther was able to complete her assignment because she forsook the title of wife and focused on her position. One of the ways to have a flourishing marriage is forgetting about the title *wife* and master being his helpmeet. As his wife, your role changes. For example, sometimes, I'm my husband's manager. My husband has a kennel business. He's great at taking care of his dogs. He's great at putting his dogs out there, but he's not great at handling conflict. With my experience in customer service, this comes easy to me. Whenever an issue arises with a customer, I handle it for him. I also handle legal stuff for him including the contracts and making sure all things are in order for a smooth sale. Don't get so comfortable with the title "wife" that you neglect to be his helpmeet. Sometimes your role has to shift so that the team can win even though your position remains the same.

I saw a demonstration of a man's brain, which was just one box, and a woman's brain that had so many different compartments and boxes in it. His box didn't need to be replaced with hers, and hers didn't need to be replaced with his. She just needed to know what box to pull from to be his helpmeet when he needed whatever he needed for the success of the team. Men are created to see the big picture and women are created with the steps necessary to help them get there. Most men do not know who they are, but the right woman will be able to help him figure it out. He's looking for someone who knows who she is and understands her position because he is looking for his helpmeet to fulfill his God- given mission.

Your Husband is Not Your Enemy

After a heated argument with my husband, I tried to get my anger under control but this particular day, I couldn't seem to override my flesh. I decided to go for a drive to calm myself down. With the radio on blast, the songs I listened to were based on my emotions at the time. As I cruised down the highway, I got to a place where I decided to no longer talk to myself and decided to talk to God. Over the radio in a booming voice, I heard God say, "Your husband is not your enemy." I heard Him, but I kept going on and on about the situation and how I wanted my husband to apologize. Finally, I went back home to my prayer room. As I began to pray, God said it again, "Your husband is not your enemy."

"What do you mean?" I asked.

"You have a true enemy who is seeking to destroy once again what I have put together. In this marriage it is you and me."

Confused by His response, I asked,"How is it you and me? Wouldn't it be, me, you, and Parnell?"

"No," He explained, "because you are no longer two but one."

That was the moment I understood the power of being one and who the real enemy is. The enemy is not your husband, but the real enemy may be using your husband to come against you because he wants to cause division in your home. He wants to kill your confidence, steal your joy, and destroy your marriage. He wants to destroy the head so the body will be uncovered. It's easier to attack the body when the head is not covering it. Our brain is the most powerful organ in our body; it controls everything. And if the brain shuts down, the body dies. When you see your husband as the enemy, the enemy will use this tactic to get you to fight against yourself because you are now one with your spouse. The enemy will use you to tear down your own household because he knows that a house divided against itself cannot stand. There will be times when you simply do not like your spouse. There will be times when your spouse will push all of the right buttons in a way that only they can. There will be times when you look at them, and you'll think they have devil horns on their head. Always remember that your husband is not your enemy. It's easy to win a war, when you remember that you're on the same team.

Stay On The Same Page

Division can creep into a marriage in the smallest ways. When my husband and I first got married, we didn't agree on anything.

If he wanted chicken, I wanted steak. If he told the kids not to go outside, I told them to go outside. If he wanted to sleep on the right side of the bed, I wanted to sleep on the right side of the bed. It was utter chaos. We didn't even agree on having our money in the same account. How crazy was it for me to trust this man with my life, have a child by him, but not trust him with my money? Even when we would visit our relatives, I would want to stay at my mother's house, and he wanted to stay at his mother's house. I didn't really trust my husband to lead, so I made all of the decisions because I felt I knew best. The constant disagreement led to division, discord, and strife.

God has a purpose and plan for your marriage. In order for this plan to be fulfilled, you and your spouse have to agree so you'll get to the same destination. In a marriage, there must be an overall common goal. This does not mean that you will always agree on the same route, but it does mean you have to agree on getting to the same destination. For example, my husband is the king of exploring new routes. This part about him would irritate me to the highest of high because in my mind, he's going the wrong way or doing something unnecessary. I remember getting so frustrated with him on the way to church one morning because he took a route that we hadn't taken before, and I just knew we were going to be late. Being late is a humongous pet peeve of mine because it shows a lack of appreciation for what others have established. It also disrupts order, which brings chaos. This particular morning, I began to rant and yell. During my ranting and yelling, we ended up at church quicker than the normal route. My husband didn't say anything, but he had a smug look on his face. "You are always trying to do something extra." I said. He replied, "But we got here on time didn't we?" The overall goal was to get to church on time. It didn't matter who got us there faster or the route that we took as long as it didn't cause division and got us where we needed to be when we needed to be there.

Agreement doesn't mean one person loses. Agreement is actually the opposite. It keeps out discord, confusion, and strife and builds trust in the marriage. Agreement means there is no "I" in team. Agreement is about making sure the overall common goal is met to reach the desired destination. When you and your spouse are a unified force, you're in agreement and there is power in agreement. Agreement brings forth the manifestation of the promises of God in your marriage.

"Again, truly I tell you that if two of you on earth agree about anything they ask for, it will be done for them by my Father in heaven."

MATTHEW 18:19 (NIV)

It's So Hard to Say Goodbye

Things began to get rocky in the beginning of our marriage when my husband found out that he would be deployed to Iraq for five months as soon as he checked into his newly assigned duty station in Fort Hood, Texas. My husband was so excited about us moving to Texas with him to start our family. On the other hand, I was terrified. I loved my husband for sure, but I had never lived away from home with a man before, neither had I ever lived away from my family to a place where I didn't know anyone. I had so many fears running through my mind. I was about to move to the biggest city I had ever lived in before with three children, and my husband would be leaving us alone for five months.

In one ear I was being encouraged by loved ones to leave, but in the other ear my fears were increased by other loved ones agreeing with my fears. My husband and I went back and forth for months about me coming. I would tell him I was coming, but when the time came, I would make an excuse as to why I couldn't come right then. I would even use our son, who was born with bronchitis, as a reason to not come down, afraid that he wouldn't make it in the Texas heat. During this time, he would come home to visit almost every weekend, driving ten hours one way. Although we enjoyed our time together, he continued to stress that he was tired of living in two separate states, taking care of two separate households when he didn't have to. This opened the door to division in our marriage, and we began to grow apart. My husband started becoming distant, not answering his phone when he was supposed to. He started staying out all night, going to the clubs and drinking. He lived his life as a married man when he was with me, and a single man when he went back to Texas. The distance and change was really taking a toll on our marriage all because I was refusing to leave and cleave (Genesis 2:24). In my mind, he was trying to take me away from my comfort zone. He was removing me from everything and everyone I had ever known. The reality is that he was trying to be obedient by becoming one with his wife. God helped me realized that it was so hard to say goodbye because I didn't understand how to become one with my husband. I was so dependent on my family. The truth is my family came before my husband. This is not how God ordained it.

Remember that your marriage is symbolic to the relationship between God and the church. This means that God comes first in your life, as should your husband. This does not mean you have to cut your family off. It just means that you respect the position of your husband and make sure that others do too. It's so important for you to make sure the people in your circle are encouraging you and holding you accountable for doing what God says to do when it comes to your marriage. Your circle greatly influences the decisions that affect your marriage. If anyone is pulling you in the opposite direction of what God has ordained, it can destroy your marriage.

Defeat Divorce Court

Warning comes before destruction. In my car, my computer system tells me digitally how many miles before I need an oil change. If the air pressure in my tires gets low, it warns me ahead of time. When my transmission was having trouble, the system told me that it could cause major problems, resulting in an accident and to take it immediately to the nearest dealership for servicing. All of these warning signs let me know that I need to take care of this problem before it causes greater damage. The warning signs in your marriage will always be there. Remember, small things become big things. The sooner you catch and address the problem, the better chance of survival. From experience, everyone has a breaking point. If I had taken his "warning signals" or concerns seriously in the beginning, a lot of the unnecessary heartache and pain could've been avoided.

It's easier to maintain a marriage than it is to restore one. The grass will always look greener on the other side when you're faced with opposition. The truth is, as long as you neglect to take care of your own, everything else will appear more beautiful to you. It's the same way when you look at a woman with a toned body, and you begin to compare your body to their body, or to what your body used to look like. Her body looks really good, but it's only because there is maintenance being done. Something will always appear more enticing to you if you're not spending time taking care of what you have. When your effort is placed on making what you already have better, it takes your focus off of other things that could lure you away, or cause you to no longer desire what you have or throw in the towel.

Now that I've been purged and prepared, I needed the tools to maintain my position. Getting to the altar is not as difficult as staying out of divorce court. It's not just enough to stay married. You want a marriage that thrives, prospers, and continues to exemplify the abundant life God promised. This section will help you do just that.

Delete the Word Divorce

"If you make divorce an option, it will become a reality."

SHAMIEKA DEAN, THE QUEEN OF RESTORATION

"Where are you going?" I yelled.

"I'm leaving." He said.

"When are you coming back?" I asked.

"I'm not. I'm done, Shamieka" as he continued walking outside.

I stood in the doorway watching him walk back and forth from the house to his silver drop-top Mustang with 20 inch rims. Each trip, he was carrying more of his belongings. My mind was racing with a thousand thoughts; my heartbreaking a thousand times.

"Satan, I rebuke you in the name of Jesus." I said to interrupt the vision I was seeing. This was the second time I had that vision. The first time I was home in my bedroom, but this time I was sitting in church trying to focus. I just knew it was Satan trying to distract me. I wish it was Satan trying to distract me. It was actually God warning me. Every time my husband and I would have a heated argument, I would ask for the "Dirty D," the seven-letter word that has become normal in our society today and should be completely deleted from your vocabulary. If the word *divorce* ever comes to your mind, toss it out. If you have to literally bite your tongue to keep from saying it, do so because that word shattered my heart into millions of pieces, and forced my children to experience a pain I could not heal. There were many incidents leading up to our divorce, but the reality was that I had been planting the seed of divorce long before it happened.

The sad truth is that when I said my vows, I really did not take them seriously. I told you that I was a single-married woman. I had one foot in the door and one foot out of the door. The history of divorce in my family was at an all-time high. In the back of my mind, I had already had my "if we ever get divorced" plan mapped out before the ink on the license was dry. The reason you must delete this word from your mind and vocabulary is because if you make divorce an option, it will become a reality. As of this day, make the decision that divorce is not an option. Make a promise right now that you will not allow this word to come out of your mouth and will always destroy the thought of divorce.

"Confess your faults one to another, and pray one for another, that ye may be healed. The effectual fervent prayer of a righteous man availeth much."

JAMES 5:16 (KJV)

Tell On Yourself

An apology is the first step in the healing process, but not the cure. If you have offended your spouse, allow them time to heal. Remember that healing is a process and the time needed to heal depends on the depth of the wound. If you attempt to rush the process, it could cause more damage. You may choose the crime, but you can't choose the time it takes the offended to heal. Although I had admitted my faults to my husband, I didn't want to face them. I wanted him to just get over the things I had done to hurt him. It was difficult for me to face my own failures because I had always pointed out my husband's faults in our marriage. I would briefly glimpse at my sins, but magnified his, even though my husband was letting me know how I made him feel weak, unappreciated, and less than a man. Instead of accepting my imperfections, I would resort to fault finding or becoming the victim.

This is another reason why revisiting your pain and healing from that pain is so important. I had to point fingers at him because he would bring my faults to light. I felt rejected and if he was right about anything, I felt like I had lost the upper hand. I needed to always be right and in control of every situation because I hadn't dealt with my issues. If you don't deal with your issues, your issues will deal with you. If you are like me, I felt as if I didn't have any faults, but your unwillingness to evaluate self can lead to disaster. The reality is that my husband was saying some of the same things to me that I had heard growing up, but I refused to acknowledge that I had issues. My mother, siblings, friends, and coworkers had always complained about how harsh and condescending my words were toward people. I always found a way to justify why I was the way that I was, without accepting responsibility and putting forth the effort to make the necessary changes.

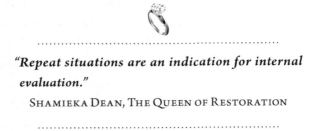

"Repeat situations are an indication for internal evaluation."

SHAMIEKA DEAN, THE QUEEN OF RESTORATION

The people who really love you will tell you the truth about yourself. Whenever you find that people who love you are saying similar things about you, it's time to evaluate to see if there is truth to what they are saying. It's easy to point out the fault in others, but it's difficult to admit our own faults. It is necessary to close the door to resentment, bitterness, unforgiveness, and retaliation, which can lead to the destruction of your marriage. Your faults may be unforgiveness, nagging, controlling, unwilling to submit, trust issues, baggage from past hurts, harsh words, withholding sex as punishment or offering it only as a reward, ineffective communication, placing other things before your spouse, unwilling to become one with your spouse, lack of support, lack of encouragement; or being a single-minded woman to name a few. No matter how small these faults may appear to you, they weigh the same in the eyes of God. It may seem insignificant to you, but the pain can be major to your spouse.

Whatever the fault may be, confess it so that you all can be healed. It's so much easier to heal when you're not walking the journey alone. It also makes it easier to forgive yourself when you aren't made to feel like you're trying to live up to the perfection of your spouse. When you acknowledge your faults, do this without justifying or pointing out the faults of your spouse. True confession is about humility and mercy. True confession apologizes without excuses. Why you did what you did doesn't matter when offering an apology, unless your spouse asks. Simply confess and apologize.

"Brothers and sisters, if someone is caught in a sin, you who live by the Spirit should restore that person gently. But watch yourselves, or you also may be tempted."
GALATIANS 6:1 (NIV)

Holding my husband hostage to his faults was so easy for me. It felt good to have one up on him, keeping him bound to his mistakes and making him feel like he owed me, until I was also tempted and fell into the same sin I stoned him for. I was so busy pointing out his failures until I wasn't wise enough to close the doors to my own temptation. I saw him as beneath me because of what he had done, yet I fell much harder than he did because I had elevated myself to a place of self-righteousness. I never thought to pray for him in those areas of weakness, until I found myself in that situation. I used to wonder how he could do what he did to me since he said he loved me, and was fully convinced that he couldn't possibly love me if he did things to hurt me. But I got my own personal experience of walking a mile in his shoes and saw how easy it was to fall into sin. I saw how powerful the generational curses are in a bloodline that aren't dealt with and how you can want so badly to do right, but still end up doing wrong.

Most importantly, I was able to understand the depth of God's grace, love, and mercy. I was able to now extend that same love, grace, and mercy to my husband as well as God had extended to me. I've learned how to become merciful and not judgmental by dealing with the "mote in my own eye" instead of being so quick to point out the speck in others. I've learned to dig deeper than what meets the eye, asking God to show me the root of a person's problems instead of condemning them for their actions. Last but not least, I've learned how to pray for his weaknesses so that I won't be tempted also.

Talk, Talk, Talk

"I know you heard me! Didn't I tell you to pick your stuff up off of the floor? You're worse than the kids. You're a grown man. You should know better. Don't worry about it. I will do it by myself." I argued.

"Shamieka, stop talking to me like a kid. I'm not a kid. You're not going to keep talking to me like that," he demanded. "If you stop acting like a kid," I yelled, "I will stop treating you like one! Matter of fact, just shut up talking to me!"

I was ashamed to type that, but it's the truth that sets you free. It's the truth that set me free. In the beginning of my marriage, my mouth was a lethal weapon. If you ever made me feel embarrassed or hurt my feelings, I would rip you to shreds with my words. One day my husband said, "You're the only person I've ever known who does not have to say one cuss word, but you can talk to a person in a way that makes them feel two feet tall." I took pride in that because it made me feel a false sense of power. If I couldn't fight you with my hands, I would beat you with my intellect and words.

Communication was a huge challenge in our marriage. As you can see, my mouth was horrific. I did not talk to my husband; I talked at him, down to him, and disrespected him even in front of others. If he didn't do things when I said do them or how I wanted them done, I turned into a degrading machine. I said whatever came to my mind without regard for his feelings. I didn't care who was around. My husband, on the other hand, was very passive. He would agree with me most of the time just to get me to be quiet. It would irritate me because I knew that's what he was doing. He did not believe in arguing, but I loved to argue. I immediately let him know when he did something I didn't like. He held his feelings inside when I did something that he didn't like. He would harbor his feelings until he finally exploded. This often caused things to come out at the wrong time and in the wrong way. He would also shut down completely when he was hurting. I would try to get him to talk about it, but he wouldn't. He was communicating in his own way and I communicated in my way, but we didn't effectively communicate with each other.

Our communication skills had always been this way; however, it was acceptable for us because it had worked in our favor until it no longer worked for us. A clear sign that it's time for change is when the things you used to do no longer work for you. I used to say we were the exact opposite, but now I say we are the perfect balance. Where I'm weak, he's strong. When I'm experiencing a storm, he's my peace. When I need to laugh, he's my comedian and vice versa. This is good news now, but initially I only saw it as his weakness, and I played heavily on it. I had absolutely no respect for my husband. I would yell at him not caring how I talked to him publicly or privately.

One day we were visiting my mother's house. We were headed out to eat and had a disagreement about something right before we got ready to leave. All of my siblings, the children, and my mother were standing in the living room as we prepared to leave the house. My husband asked me a question and I yelled back, "Shut up talking to me." I would never forget the pain in his eyes as he stood there with embarrassment all over his face. I destroyed his manhood and his ego. I diminished him in front of everyone. My mom said, "You are going to lose a good man if you don't change the way you talk to him." I was hurting because I hurt him, but I was so filled with pride, I didn't take the chance to correct it. My conscious was beaten down all night. I apologized and although he accepted my apology, the pain was still there. It took years to repair the damage I had done in that moment.

When you think of communication, what is the first definition to come to mind? It's probably talking. For me communication had one purpose—to get my point across. I needed to be heard—whether I was heard through words or behavior—I was going to be heard. According to Merriam Webster, *communication is the act or process of using words, sounds, signs, or behaviors to express or exchange information or to express your ideas, thoughts, feelings, etc., to someone else,* which means it isn't always verbal communication. We communicate in various ways. In today's society, text messaging and social media is one of the highest forms of communication. My personal preference is to text but experience has proved it is not the best method of communication. I've had some very bad misunderstandings using text and email, because depending on the mood of the person or the relationship you have with that person, the message can be taken in a completely different way than you intended it.

With most women, body language is our way of communicating. We can let a man know if we are angry, ready for love, excited or having a visit from mother nature strictly with our body language. Have you said one thing with your mouth, but your actions showed another? You're smiling but your body language is screaming anger? How about the infamous silent treatment? I was the queen of silent treatment in my marriage. I did it because I knew it made my husband upset. He would try to talk to me, and I would stare him in the face without mumbling a word. For years, it worked. He would cave because he hated to feel ignored. Secretly, I enjoyed it because it made me feel in control. If I wasn't playing the silent treatment, I communicated by denying sex when I got mad. If that didn't work, I would yell like a tyrant.

This created a barrier in our marriage. He got tired of playing games and would shut down. I was so focused on getting my way that I went to whatever length to get it, until it no longer worked in my favor. When all I knew to get what I wanted failed, I was forced to look in the mirror to understand what communication was. Communication is an exchange of information but just exchanging information does not provide solutions when problems arise in a marriage. Communication in your marriage has to be effective. The purpose of effective communication is to find a solution that works for all parties involved. In order to do this, you must listen to each other. Remember, listen and silent have the same letters because you must do one to do the other. You have to be silent to listen. You are not listening to respond; you are listening to understand. You need to understand their feelings and actions to learn how to communicate with them in a way that they understand.

One of the biggest mistakes most couples make is ignoring the little signs. Listen to your spouse and don't disregard their frustrations no matter how small or insignificant they may seem to you. If they voiced them to you then it means a lot to them. Unresolved small matters become huge issues that help you fast track your way to divorce court. The elephant in the room won't go away because you refuse to face it. In every marriage, challenges will present themselves. It may not be anything major, but no matter what it is, you want to quickly and effectively deal with any problems so that they will not fester. Suppressing the issues will only cause them to explode when the right amount of pressure is placed on them. Don't disregard the things your spouse has a problem with. Really seek to understand where they are coming from.

Just a Little Bit—Respect

I remember belting out the words to the hit song "Respect" by Aretha Franklin as a young one. I didn't realize just how important that word was when it came to men. It validates his strength as a man and his position as a leader. When a man is disrespected, it makes him feel weak and powerless. Respect is one of the ways a woman says to her husband, "I love you" and "I trust you." A man always wants to be the hero to his household and a lot of how he feels inside comes from how he sees himself in his wife's eyes.

Believe it or not, men have just as many insecurities as women. Unlike women, they are not good at expressing themselves or highlighting their insecurities because they have been made to believe that it is a weakness to do so. Men compete just as much, if not more, than women. The testosterone you see in the gym. The muscle flexing. The competitive sports. The fancy cars, beautiful women, high paying jobs are all ways for men to get respect. None of those things amount to anything if they do not get the respect in their home. If the one he's called to protect doesn't respect him, it damages him more than anything else. He needs to be able to trust safely in you (Proverbs 31:11), and as a wife, you set the tone for the level of respect he will receive outside of his home for others. He has to not only be able to trust you to be loyal to him, but also in his dreams, challenges, and passions. I want to go back to the story of Queen Vashti to highlight how a lack of respect from a wife to her husband can cause trouble. When Queen Vashti refused to come before King Xerxes as he asked her to, he had a meeting with the leaders in the community. They immediately let the King know that because of Queen Vashti's position of influence, her actions would cause a domino effect on every other woman in the community. Basically, if she lead by the example of disrespecting the head of her household, the other women would do the same thing. If a man cannot effectively manage his own family, how can he manage anything else (1 Timothy 3:5 NIV).

Don't Make God a Competitor

"You spend more time at the church than you spend at home with me," he spewed. Furious, I yelled back, "You act like I'm out in the streets all night. I'm trying to serve God. I'm at the church six days a week, trying to live my life right, and you're complaining about that. What man in their right mind would get mad at their wife for serving God?"

"You can say what you want to say Shamieka, but God is not the one that has you at that church six days a week," he rebutted. I ended the conversation by refusing to respond.

In my mind, I thought he was losing his mind and this was grounds for divorce for sure because there was no way I was putting this man before *my* God.

I had allowed Satan to convince me that my husband was trying to come between my relationship with God. I told God I would sacrifice everything for Him, my husband included. The following day, I was on the phone with a friend of mine explaining the argument my husband and I had. Thankfully, she did not give me the response I was hoping for. She gave me a response that helped change the course of my marriage and my life. "Listen to what your husband is saying," she advised. "He feels like he's competing with God for his wife." I replayed the conversation between my husband and me repeatedly over the next three or four hours when it finally hit me. My husband was letting me know in his own way that I was choosing church over him. I didn't say God because I realized that I wasn't choosing God, the church had become my idol. In addition to my full-time position as an assistant manager at the bank and transporting my children to soccer, football and step team practice, I was also over the youth praise team at my church. I was on the media team, vice president of the choir, attending Sunday school, Bible study, and regular worship service every week.

My schedule included everything except for being a wife to my husband. My heart was in the right place and my intentions were good, but my home was out of order. I failed to realize that my most important ministry was my home. Men are already territorial, so don't ever make your spouse feel like they are in competition with God. If he feels like God is pulling you away from him, he'll resent you and the God you serve. Make sure the things you take on in ministry are not just good works, but God-given assignments.

Be His Wife Not His Minister

I made the mistake that many Christian women make who are sold out to God and want so desperately for their husbands to be on the same page. I became his minister instead of being his wife. I no longer had a conversation with my husband, I became a walking bible. Everything that came out of my mouth was scripture or God. I used the word of God in a way that was not edifying but condemning.

"You know better. You were raised in the church."

"God is going to whip you better than I can."

"You're supposed to be a man of God."

"God don't like ugly."

"If you keep playing with God, you're going to burst hell wide open."

"You need to get your life right with God."

"You think God is going to bless you and you're acting like that?"

"You need to be delivered."

These were the words I spewed at my husband on a consistent basis. The word of God should never be used as a weapon against your spouse. Your representation of God will either draw your husband closer to God or push him farther away from God. Your husband can be preached to at church, through the television, radio, or a podcast station. As an imitator of Christ, your reflection should resemble the actions that will cause him to want what you have. Think about it. Who would want to serve someone who's always reminding them of their failures, tearing them down, or threatening them with damnation? Remember, love is an action that must be shown. If you can't win him with your actions, your words won't make a difference. Be his wife, not his minister.

Be His Cheerleader

I posted our family photos on Facebook and a young lady commented, "You look so happy. I wish I had a husband like yours." I did not do this publicly, but I reached out to her to let her know that she should never compare her husband to another man. If you always tell a child they are bad, they will make that their identity, doing what is expected of them. This is the same way with your husband. If he knows you expect him to fail and you continue to speak failure over his life, he will fail.

I remember watching a sixteen second video clip of Stephen Curry, a professional basketball player named NBA MVP 2014-2015, walking to the locker room after his team had taken a loss. You could see the discouragement on his face with each step. This look immediately turned from gloom to glow when he looked to his left. There his wife was standing in the hallway with confetti in her hand. She tossed it into the air as he walked through. She was his cheerleader even in a moment of defeat. She could've compared his game to the other team. She could've pointed out his mistakes, but she chose to celebrate him instead. This is what I mean by being his biggest cheerleader. If her husband opens the doors for her and yours don't, you better applaud your husband on how good he cuts the grass. You should always be his biggest cheerleader with your pom poms and bullhorn on standby. No one in the bleachers should ever shout louder than the one he's become one with. No matter how many weaknesses your husband has, magnify his strengths while praying for his shortcomings. Even if he isn't good enough for others, make sure he knows that he's good enough for you. God is not going to give you a perfect husband, but He will give you the one who's perfect for you. When one member is struggling, the other teammate steps up to the plate. It is about the team.

Toot His Horn

The whole world was watching one of the biggest competitions in the world when world-renowned comedian and talk show host, Steve Harvey called out the wrong name for the Miss Universe pageant. The look of failure and devastation took over his face when he realized he announced the wrong contestant. Steve immediately took responsibility for his actions, but it did not stop the entire world from crashing down on him. Every TV show, social media platform, and radio station was headlining this horrible mistake. Imagine having everyone in the world watch you utterly fail and crushing the hearts of others in the process.

No matter how much he apologized, they kept throwing daggers at him. Of course he had to address it on his talk show, and the ratings for that episode were at an all-time high. After he continuously apologized and attempted to rectify the situation, they asked him how he managed to remain positive throughout this ordeal. "I can deal with the world calling me a failure. But as long as I know I'm still a hero in Marjorie's eyes, I can make it." Steve said. Marjorie, his wife, posted a photo edifying him in the face of the world. She stood with him when he fell short and encouraged him so that he could get back up. In his lowest moment, she was his mountain top.

Edification is one of those methods of communication that gives Clark Kent the powers to be Superman. I had several women in disbelief ask me why I called my husband, my king. They looked at me as if I were crazy. I called him "king" because I was speaking to where he was going, not where he was. My husband was not always acting like a king. But once I learned the power of my words, I began to speak to who God said he was until he rose to the occasion. The reason your words will cause more damage to your husband than anyone else ever will is because of your position in his life. A woman was created from the rib of a man, making you a part of him. The rib was created to protect the heart, so don't crush the heart you were created to protect. This is the ultimate form of betrayal because you're the closest one to him.

If you want to see a man rise to the occasion every time, respect him and edify him. Let him know that you have his back no matter what. The whole world may turn against him, but as long as he has the support of you, he'll be okay.

Say Thanks

Appreciation goes out of the door when obligation takes its place. Oftentimes, we don't feel the need to say thank you simply because we feel like our spouses are obligated to do certain things. There is a mentality of why we should thank or reward them for doing what a husband is supposed to do. It may be what they are supposed to do, but the reality is, they do not have to do it. When I'm tempted to complain about something I feel he should have done, I remind myself of all the things he's already done throughout the week. Things as simple as taking the trash out to the road, fixing me a cup of coffee, or picking up his socks get a "thank you." A person who's appreciated will always do more. It also shows your spouse that you are not taking advantage of them.

Don't Forsake "I Love You"

I was desperately craving my husband's attention, but he was busy with another one of his projects. This particular project had been going on for over a week. My patience was running thin with being the normal supportive wife I usually am. Instead of me telling him I wanted his attention, I developed a nasty attitude toward him. Unbothered by my obvious frustration, he continued working on his project. My temperature rose an additional 350 degrees, and I stormed off appalled by his choice to ignore my desperate need of affection. *He's been married to me long enough to know what's wrong with me,* I thought. With each passing second, I got angrier. Nighttime quickly approached. He walked into our bedroom after a long, hot shower, attempting to start a conversation as if everything was okay, but I completely ignored him. Aware that his actions weren't working, he leaned over me, pressed his lips against my cheek and whispered, "I love you, babe." Angrily, I rolled over without a response, slid as far away from him as possible and eventually fell asleep.

The next morning I saw a look in his eyes that alarmed me. I couldn't understand why tears were clouding those beautiful puppy dog eyes. Fear gripped my heart as I sat up on the side of the bed. "Babe, are you okay? I asked. "What's wrong?" His head dropped and a tear rolled slowly down his left cheek. Panic is an understatement of the emotion running through my mind. My palms began sweating profusely as I proceeded to walk toward him. I gently placed my hands on the side of his face, allowing his face to rest safely in my palms. "What happened?" I asked. A stream of tears began pouring from his eyes. "I woke up this morning and all I could think about is how we went to bed angry," his voice trembled, "and one of us could've died."

Just the thought of it had my heart in so much pain I couldn't breathe. "You didn't even respond when I told you 'I loved you,'" he continued. "Don't ever do that again." As I marinated on what he said, I felt guilty and ashamed as my heart sank. My pettiness and immaturity could've left either of us with a lifetime of regret. I apologized to my husband and told him I loved him until he got tired of me saying it. So, don't ever forsake "I love you" even if you're upset with your spouse. You don't ever want to live with the regret of an argument being the last words you ever say to your spouse.

Love Him Right

One of the most powerful life-changing books I've ever read, that helped my marriage was the *5 Love Languages* by Dr. Gary Chapman. This book helped me to understand so much about myself and my husband. I don't know about you, but I had love all wrong. My definition of love was that I got everything I wanted when I wanted. It was that warm and fuzzy feeling in my stomach that made everything easy. I thought love was being showered with gifts, and if a person loved me, they would do whatever I told them to do when I told them to do it. This was not necessarily love, but this was definitely my love language. According to the quiz in Dr. Gary Chapman's book, my love language is receiving gifts and acts of service, which is why I only felt loved when someone was buying me gifts and doing things for me. My husband didn't know that about me. He was a nice man, but he didn't understand why I would be so irate when he didn't get me a gift or when he wouldn't do what I asked him to do. In his eyes, love was making sure the bills were paid and taking care of things that were tore up around the house, but I could care less about those things when it came to me feeling loved.

My husband's love language is words of affirmation and quality time. After reading the book, it really helped me understand why my negative remarks to him would hurt him so deeply. It would deeply bother him when I didn't want to be affectionate. Most women would probably be extremely happy to hold hands while walking in the park, cuddling with their husband while watching a movie, or having their husband around them a lot. I'm the exact opposite. This type of behavior for me was smothering because affection was not a way that I felt loved.

This brings me to the question: Is our love language based on things we were deprived of growing up or because of an incident in our past that made us desire those things? When I was growing up, I was rejected by both parents. I also was forced to be an adult well before I should've been. My mom worked two or three jobs most of the time and my stepfather was never home, so I was responsible for taking care of my siblings. I had to feed, clothe, bathe, comb hair, help with homework, and do all of this for myself also (and remember, I had my first child at fifteen). I always had to do for others, but no one took care of me. I never got any appreciation for it. When my husband was growing up, he was called derogatory names by his parents and siblings and made to feel like he wasn't smart enough. His parents were always gone away from home, and he didn't receive any affection from them. The areas that we were damaged in often become our greatest need for love. Until we are taught that each person feels love differently, we love them the way we want to be loved. I would be so hurt when my husband wasn't as excited as I was about the gifts I bought him. It was an insult to me because I was trying to show him I loved him, and he wasn't receiving it the way I expected him to. On the flip side, if he wanted to take me out for dinner for my birthday, I wouldn't be excited. Instead, I would've loved a thoughtful gift or him cooking my favorite meal at home.

Now that I know his love language, I will gladly give him a massage or plan an event doing something he loves like fishing.

My husband is also good with his hands and loves to build and repair things. I could care less how things are made; however, I surprise him by coming to watch as he builds things, even asking questions to show interest. Although I do not like these things, he told me it makes him feel good that I do because I know he likes it. In return, he does things for me like clean the bedroom or cook without me asking.

Learning how you receive love is important so that you can communicate it to your husband. But learning how he receives love is equally important so you'll be able to love him the right way.

Keep It Sizzling

First things first, don't get complacent. Marriage is not the time to take things for granted. Don't let yourself go simply because you've made it to the altar. My grandmother used to say, "The same thing you did to get him, do it to keep him." Let's start with the basics. Ladies, your husband shouldn't feel like he's rubbing legs with another hairy man. There is a reason we were created delicately. Our hands are softer than men and our scent is sweeter than men. A man likes a woman who is soft and smells good. Make sure you're handling the basics of shaving, staying moisturized, and smelling fresh.

Comfort kills intimacy, so by any means necessary, keep your husband lusting after you. Ladies, I know we love to be comfortable. I do too. I am a fuzzy socks, pajama, onesie loving woman. The older the pajamas the more comfortable they are. We all have our go-to clothing that we feel so comfortable in:

the holey, oversized T-shirt, worn-out socks, and the bonnet are just a few of those comfort clothing items. I'm a bonnet woman myself, but that bonnet, along with the other comfy items, has a time and a place, which is post intimacy.

I know as a mother, career woman, and wife, being sexy is not always a priority on our list. Children greatly affect our bodies and make us feel unattractive. After my third child, I completely lost my sex appeal. I gained weight and just didn't feel sexy at all. Lingerie was a no-no and I found myself complaining a lot about my appearance. Even after my husband would compliment me, I felt so unattractive that I wouldn't receive his compliments. I remember hearing Joseph Prince, Senior, Pastor of New Creation Church in Singapore say, "Don't paint that negative image of yourself to your husband. It can cause him to see you in the negative image you've given him." I didn't realize that I was now painting a negative image to him with my words. I stopped doing that immediately. My unhappiness would eventually rub off on my husband, and I couldn't allow that to happen. Although I was still beautiful to my husband, I had to be comfortable in my own skin. I started working out three times a week, and changed a couple of my eating habits.

If you are unhappy with your appearance and you can do something to change it, do so. Complaining about it only magnifies it, and whatever you magnify, you intensify. Make this change for yourself because when you look good, you feel good. Stock up on your sexy apparel. You can keep a very limited supply of comfort clothing, but only wear them during that certain "time of the month" or post intimacy. When it's that time of the month, comfort is perfectly okay (I'm sure your husband will agree). However, do not use your comfort clothing as "don't touch me" clothing. If you don't want to do lingerie, your birthday suit is always a winner. Skin to skin contact also increases sexual arousal and intensifies intimacy.

Sex toys. Yes, let's talk about it. I was always taught to be a lady in the streets, and please him in the sheets. I'm all for keeping it spicy in the bedroom. It can get a bit of a drag after being together for years and life takes its toll on you. There is nothing wrong with using something to enhance the sexual pleasure between the two of you. When I say enhancers, I'm talking about lotions, lubricants, smell goods, good music, candles, and so on. Inviting sex toys into your bedroom, that take the place of what your husband was born with, is a no-no. There should not be anything that could replace the equipment God gave your husband. A man cannot compete with something that he feels minimizes his size or that goes faster than he could on his best day. Remember to enhance not replace. The marriage bed is undefiled, but it doesn't mean the bed should be made impure. Nothing satisfies a man's ego more than knowing he's satisfying his wife in the bedroom.

Two of the most overlooked things in maintaining intimacy and keeping the spice in your sex life are exercising and what you eat. Exercising not only keeps you in shape, but it boosts your confidence by physically looking good. And hearing your husband compliment you on your gorgeous physique is always a plus. According to Dr. Laura Berman from *Everyday*

Health, "Regular exercise boosts circulation, tones the body, and primes the brain for sexual satisfaction." Proper blood flow improves arousal because it provides better lubrication and the sensation to your genitals, which increase your sexual excitement. Exercise is a major factor for sexual pleasure for women because it relaxes the mind, taking away the stress that we deal with daily. As you know, women are satisfied more mentally, so regular exercise will help you get mentally prepared to enjoy intercourse. Women are more mentally stimulated than anything and regular exercise routine helps your mind to relax so that your body can too. I'm sure you've heard the saying, "You are what you eat," and this is so painfully true because the foods you eat greatly impact your sexual desire, which negatively impacts the intimacy in your marriage.

Think about fast food. According to Health.com, "Many fried and fast foods have high levels of 'bad fats,' such as saturated and trans fat, which can negatively affect your heart and impede blood flow due to a buildup of fatty plaque in the arteries." Fast food is not only unhealthy for us, but it also affects our energy level, which then affects our mood. When you do not eat the right things, you'll feel groggy, moody, and unattractive. Grumpy, lazy sex is a real turn off and most of the time, we think that as long as we give it to him, he will be satisfied. That is such a myth. Men want to feel like you're attracted to them, and a man who really loves his wife does not want her to make him feel like he's forcing her, that she's not into it, or that she's just another woman on the street. According to Health.com, foods such as strawberries, avocado, almonds, sweet potatoes, sesame seed, and watermelon increases blood flow and libido action, which makes your sex life more satisfying.

Positioning Yourself to be a Wife is also about learning how to play your position by knowing when to switch up your role. Remember your position remains the same, but sometimes your role has to change. For example, sometimes, I'm his girlfriend. I make sure I keep myself looking sexy for him. There are times when I'll just throw on a cute little black dress without plans to go out. Sometimes being a wife doesn't feel sexy because of the tasks that come along with it. Most women take the title wife so seriously it takes the fun out of marriage. Sometimes you have to switch that role and be his girlfriend. Girlfriends tend to be more fun because you're in the do-whatever-to-please each-other stage, which leads me to the next point, dating. Dating should be mandatory, not optional.

When you think date, it doesn't always have to be something fancy or extravagant. A date can be as simple as having lunch together, a picnic in your bedroom after the children have gone to bed for the night, or a late night drive to the park. Make a list of date ideas so that you can plan them in advance. You don't want to take the fun out of trying to think of things at the last minute. Keep it adventurous and try something new, but always remember to keep your spouse's love language in mind.

Date ideas:

- Dinner
- Dancing
- Concert
- Picnic in the park
- Picnic for lunch
- Live band
- Tickets to see your favorite comedian
- Plays
- Couples cooking class
- Couples painting class
- Couples massage
- Private dinner at home
- Game night
- Tickets to see your favorite sports team
- Movie night
- Scenic drive
- Walk in the park
- Trip to the beach
- Ride go carts
- Go to an arcade
- Visit a theme park
- Visit a museum

With that being said, don't stop flirting with each other either. Send a flirty text, or leave a flirty note in his vehicle for him to find when he leaves for work. Keep his eyes and thoughts on you. If you prepare his lunch, put a nice, sexy picture in his lunch. Do your homework and study your spouse to see what turns them on. Don't play guessing games, and don't ever think that satisfying your spouse is a one-size-fits all. What worked for your ex might not work for your spouse, so ask him if you can't figure it out. Communicate your sexual desires clearly to your spouse and whatever you do, don't turn intimacy into a task. Make it a never-ending journey of exploration, a habit to find out more things about your spouse and how to satisfy each other. Intimacy is not just sex. Intimacy is about knowing your spouse on a much deeper level, learning more about each other as you grow and change together.

Over the years, sex drives can change. If the desire for sex begins to change, be honest about why you no longer desire sex, deal with it immediately, and don't let it fester. If you don't know why, get help to prevent opening the door for pornography, perversion, or infidelity. Don't give up!

Execute Your Strategy

"I'm tired of praying. No matter how hard I pray, things remain the same. I'm praying, but You're not answering me. You're not listening to me. God, why aren't You doing anything? Do You hear me? I'm praying like You told me to. Why should I keep praying when You're going to do what You want to do anyway?" I cried out in frustration.

Have you ever felt like your prayers are hitting the ceiling? Have you ever felt like you don't know what to pray or felt your prayers were useless? Insanity is doing the same thing expecting a different result. When it came to my marriage, I was still praying the same way. I ranted to God, telling Him about all that my husband did, as if He didn't already know. I told Him that if He only changed this about my husband, then things would be better. My husband wasn't changing, and I got tired of praying. I can be a tad bit spoiled sometimes. At least that's what I've been told. Of course, a spoiled person wouldn't agree. After all, who doesn't want what they want, when they want it, right?

I felt I had prayed long and hard enough to begin seeing the changes in my husband. I was fed up and either something was going to shake, or I was done with it all. God was not working His power fast enough, so I had my fit and told God exactly how I felt about this situation. "If he's not changing, could it be that the change needs to start with you?" was the rhetorical question God used to silence me, causing me to dig deeper. With that being said, never pray for the change in your spouse without stopping to examine yourself. This is one of the most common errors in marriage. We are quick to pray for the change we deem necessary in our spouses, completely bypassing the fact that we need those prayers for ourselves. If you're praying for your spouse and nothing is changing, stop and ask God what is it that He's trying to change in you. Could it be that God is trying to teach you longsuffering, unconditional love, and selflessness or to value your husband's strengths instead of magnifying his weaknesses?

Many times God allows us to hit a stumbling block to make us look inward. Once I dealt with myself, the strategy was revealed for me to pray effectively for my husband. James 5:16 says the "effective fervent prayers of a righteous man that availeth much." I told you earlier that the real enemy is not your husband. The real enemy doesn't attack without a plan. He studies us daily to see what makes us upset, discouraged, fearful, and faithless. When it comes to prayer, especially for your husband and marriage, you have to be strategic and not pray amiss. If you want to know when it's time to change your strategy, it's when what you used to do no longer works. Each situation causes for a different level of prayer. I'm going to focus on eight areas in which the enemy attacks men the most, giving you strategic prayers for each.

Let this mind be in you, which was also in Christ Jesus. It's important to pray that your husband has the mind of Christ because if he thinks like Christ, he will act like Christ. If he acts like Christ, he will love like Christ and lead like Christ (Philippians 2:5 KJV).

Remember, where the mind goes, the man follows. The very first prayer God gave me was to pray for my husband's mind. This is where every battle begin and every war is won.

PRAYER FOR HIS MIND. Father, let the mind of Christ Jesus be in my husband. Purify his thoughts and renew his mind whenever he tries to revert to any thought not imparted by You. Help him to immediately capture every thought that would lead him astray. Help him to accurately discern when the thoughts are not from You. Daily, let him fill his mind with Your word. Let his ears and eyes, which are the gateway to his soul, remain clear of demonic thoughts that would lead to demonic activity. Quicken his spirit if he reads, watches or listens to anything that would open the gateway for strongholds. Break any stronghold from his mind. In Jesus' name, Amen.

"Blessed are those who hunger and thirst for righteousness, for they will be filled."

MATTHEW 5:6 (NIV)

A relationship with God is most important because it is the very foundation of your marriage. The relationship your husband has with God will greatly impact how he deals with you and every other aspect of his life. It is about relationship, not religion. Be mindful that every person learns and grows at a different pace. Don't compare your relationship with God to his relationship with God. He will learn and grow on his own. If you try to rush his process or make him feel that you're spiritually superior to him, it will push him further away from God, causing him to resent God. This was something I learned the hard way. I assumed my husband would be growing at the same pace I did in my relationship with God. When he wasn't,

I became extremely frustrated and used the word of God as a weapon to tear him down. God's word and ways always edify. Patience is a virtue, and is certainly one you'll learn during this process.

PRAYER FOR HIS RELATIONSHIP WITH GOD. Father, increase my husband's desire to have an intimate relationship with You. Give him a desire for a lifestyle of praise and worship. Give him a hunger and thirst for more of You. Help him grow from faith to faith. Increase his understanding of Your word. Help him to rightly divide Your word and apply it to his life. Give him quality over quantity time with You. Give him deeper revelation of You. Show him the depth of Your love for him. When he has a problem, let him come quickly to You even if he falls short. Keep his passion for a relationship with You alive and exciting. In Jesus' name, Amen.

"Do not be misled: Bad company corrupts good character."

1 CORINTHIANS 15:33 (NIV)

Those who your husband associate with will greatly impact him. Birds of a feather flock together, so you want to pray that he's associated with people who have the same Godly standards as he does.

PRAYER FOR HIS CIRCLE OF INFLUENCE. Father, surround my husband with Godly influence. Surround him with leaders he can trust and that can be trusted. Surround him with husbands who understand their role and who love their wife as Christ loves the church. Surround him with wisdom, knowledge, and power. Surround him with those who will keep him accountable. Surround him with men who are after Your own heart. Surround him with those he has no problem allowing to lead him. Help him to see trouble, resist it, and flee quickly. In Jesus' name, Amen.

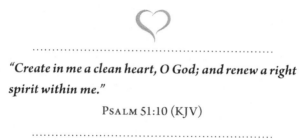

"Create in me a clean heart, O God; and renew a right spirit within me."

PSALM 51:10 (KJV)

I remember David and Tamela Mann, celebrity Christian couple, saying one of their prayers was that they only lust after each other. Contrary to popular belief, our eyes don't get saved just because we do. Some women find a man who's already in a relationship more attractive. Have you ever seen the guy in high school everyone overlooked until he got with someone else? That happens after high school too. But there are constant temptations that will come against your husband. Cover him in those areas as well because you never know when or how the temptation will attack. We don't always know how strong our husband is in certain areas, so it is important to always cover the known areas of weakness that many men have.

PRAYER FOR HIS PURITY OF HEART. Father, give my husband a pure heart. Give him a heart that lusts only after me. Give him a forgiving heart, so that his heart will never grow cold toward me, that his love for me will always flow freely. Keep him free from ungodly lusts and spirits of perversion. Guard his ear gates and eye gates from anything that will lure him away from his marriage. Give him the strength to resist any temptation speedily. In Jesus' name, Amen

"Wisdom is the principal thing; therefore get wisdom: and with all thy getting get understanding."

PROVERBS 4:7 (KJV)

It's easy to fail at something you don't understand. He needs to have a good understanding of his position and the importance of it so that he will understand how to operate in it and function to the fullest extent of his capabilities. This will also help him to not see submission as a position of slavery or entitlement from his wife. It will show him how to respect her and view her as his helpmeet and not his doormat.

PRAYER FOR UNDERSTANDING HIS ROLE AS HUSBAND. Father, give my husband complete understanding of his position as a husband. Guide him every step of the way in every decision that he has to make concerning his household. Help me to support his position and respect it. Give him in-depth wisdom as a husband, and help him to always take his role seriously. Help him to succeed in his role as a husband, and be a positive example for other husbands. When he doesn't know what to do, quicken his spirit to seek You. When he feels inadequate, unworthy, or lost in his position, give me the words to encourage him. Make him a great leader as he is the first line of defense as the head of our household. Help him to operate in the power and authority You've entrusted him with. In Jesus' name, Amen.

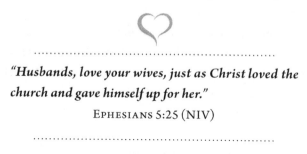

"Husbands, love your wives, just as Christ loved the church and gave himself up for her."
EPHESIANS 5:25 (NIV)

God tells women to submit and husbands to love because with men it doesn't come natural to them as it does us. Women are natural nurturers, and are more in tune with our emotions than men are. Some men didn't have a healthy view of love growing up and don't automatically know how to love like we do.

PRAYER FOR HIS ABILITY TO LOVE. Father, give my husband a heart like Yours for me. Teach him how to love accurately. Let his love for me not be self-seeking, but according to Your word. Remove any wrong teaching or examples of love he may have been taught in his past. Give him a love that is sacrificial and selfless. Purify his heart to love me like You love the church. In Jesus' name, Amen.

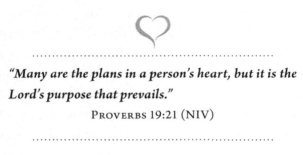

"Many are the plans in a person's heart, but it is the Lord's purpose that prevails."
PROVERBS 19:21 (NIV)

It is important for a man to know his purpose. If not, he will shoot aimlessly in life, become unfulfilled, and seek to have that void filled in other ways. A purpose-driven life brings forth passion, and passion will help him to persevere even in the times when things get tough.

PRAYER FOR HIS UNDERSTANDING OF HIS PURPOSE. Father, help my husband to uncover his purpose and unleash his potential for unlimited success in unorthodox ways. Remove any false identities, inaccurate labels, or generational strongholds that will hinder him from fulfilling his God-given purpose. Give him clarity, focus, and perseverance. Remove any fear or mental blocks that will cause him to minimize his greatness. In Jesus' name, Amen.

"Christ hath redeemed us from the curse of the law, being made a curse for us: for it is written, Cursed [is] every one that hangeth on a tree."

GALATIANS 3: 13 (KJV)

In every family, there are certain things passed along from generation to generation. Some of those things are good, some of them are not so good. It is imperative that you know what generational behaviors have been passed down to your husband, so that your prayers can be strategic in targeting those areas. If you notice behavior of older generations that are not a part of his God-given lineage, those are areas you need to pray about.

PRAYER AGAINST GENERATIONAL CURSES. Father, I pray against every generational curse that is not like You. Every word curse that has been spoken over my husband's life be reversed. I speak against the spirit of adultery, lying, addiction, abandonment. Restore my husband's God-given identity. Let his behavior line up in obedience with Your statutes. Teach him Your ways and Your truth about who he is and how he should act. Do not allow him to be entangled again with any generational curses that have come as a result of his lineage because he has been redeemed. Help him to realize and accept his freedom from generational curses and stand firm in his new identity in You. In Jesus' name, Amen.

Strategic Prayer of Sustainability for Your Marriage

Father, teach me how to operate effectively in my role as a wife. Teach my husband to operate effectively in his role as a husband. Help us to understand and fulfill the mission for our marriage. Keep our minds and hearts pure toward You and each other. Help us to operate continuously in humility, being quick to forgive each other's offenses. Unify us in every area of our marriage. Let us always keep You first in our marriage. Let our love for each other grow daily. Let our respect for one another never leave. Let the words we speak edify, encourage, and build. Let us not go to sleep angry. Let our eyes continue to find the beauty in each other. Never let divorce be an option for us so that it will not become a reality. Let us always be friends and our date life never cease.

Help me daily to submit unto my husband as unto You, and that my husband loves me as Christ loves the church. Let us focus on each other's strengths and help each other in our weaknesses. When we fall short, let us extend grace and mercy toward each other as You continuously extend mercy and grace to us in our time of need. Let us be each other's biggest cheerleaders. Let us listen to understand. Give us effective communication skills. Let our marriage be built and sustained on honesty. If we hurt each other, give us Godly sorrow, and the desire and will to fix it. Help us quickly learn from our mistakes, not to repeat them. Help us to keep you as the foundation of our marriage. Help us not to figure out things on our own but to always consult You so that You can direct our path. Teach us how to first love You. Show us how much You love us and strengthen us to love each other as You have loved us. In Jesus' name, Amen.

....

You've just read a story of restoration. A story of truth. A story of hope. Because I stand by what I preach, I wanted to share my truth with you. My marriage was not your average fairytale. I'm sure many of you are surprised by what you have read, but it is my truth that lead to restoration. I wholeheartedly believe that God can't heal what you refuse to face. When you don't deal with issues of your past, those issues will one day deal with you. It's not a matter of *if*, but a matter of *when*.

What I realized during my divorce process, is that I wasn't a wife. I was a woman who took on a man's last name. I was a woman who had forgiven those who hurt me, but didn't deal with the aftermath of the pain they caused me. I was a woman seeking validation through marriage, a woman seeking to prove a point to the ones who left me bruised, battered, and broken. No matter how long you pretend, cover up or suppress your issues, they will eventually surface. The childhood tragedies, generational curses, implanted fears, false identity, fabricated strength, and low self-esteem found their home in my marriage. Wholeness should be your intentions prior to saying, "I do" because if not, "I do" will become your identity and can destroy you.

One of my biggest inspirations in writing this book and the success of my marriage is Steve Harvey. I admire Mr. Harvey so much, not because he's a celebrity. As a matter of fact, many people condemn anyone listening to him because he gives relationship advice but has had failed marriages in the past. Society will say, "Why listen to someone who's failed?" And I say, "Why not?" Why not listen to someone who has traveled the road, took their negative experiences, learned from them, and is now teaching others to do the same? I wanted to share with you an inside look of the types of battles that can happen in your marriage, and I believe that prevention is the best method for sustainability.

When you're prepared for a storm, you can stand through it. To say we can't learn from someone who's failed, is to say that no one has the right to teach anything because every person who's now successful has failed in the areas they are now successful. The old saying, "Experience is the best teacher" is true, but you don't have to experience it for yourself. You can learn from my experiences just as I did from Steve Harvey because my naked truth has now become a guide of preparation and sustainability for successful, happy, and healthy marriages.

Epilogue

Where Are We Now?

*I*t's 7:15a.m. on a Saturday morning. The sun is lightly peeking through the windows, as the smell of bacon saturates the air. The microwave timer is going off, and I hear the sound of his voice. "Babe, breakfast is ready." We are celebrating my thirty-fifth birthday in Miami. My heart smiles as I'm in awe of God restoring our marriage after divorce. You read that right! My husband and I remarried June 11, 2012, and on September 14, 2012, we renewed our vows in front of all of our loved ones. As I walked down the aisle with my stomach doing flips, my palms sweating and my legs trembling, I wondered, *How do I know things will be better? How do I know if he's changed? How do I know this is God? What if he hasn't changed? What if I haven't changed? Will things be better this time?*

As he lifted my veil, our eyes locked, and tears were falling slowly down his face. He must've sensed my nervousness because with certainty in his voice, he whispered, "I love you." It was that moment that assurance me I was making the right decision. Everything felt right. Everything was just like I had petitioned God for it to be. I knew I was staring into the eyes of a man who knew me completely and loved me unconditionally. I knew I was no longer the broken woman afraid to let him love me. I knew I was no longer the woman afraid to submit. I was positioned to be a wife.

Each day we live to intentionally show each other how grateful we are for a second chance. There isn't a day that goes by that we don't tell each other we love each other. We date weekly, no matter what's going on. We effectively communicate our disagreements, keep God first, and divorce is no longer an option. We strategically pray together and know how to love each other the right way. We are living out our purpose. I'm now a relationship coach, author, speaker and entrepreneur. I founded A Mile in My Shoes, The Movement, which is a women's empowerment organization of over two thousand women. My husband is an audio engineer, guitarist, media director of our church, and founder of Deano Line Bullies and Tennessee Bullies. We established an institution called Real Love Rocks where we are making marriages great again. Our three areas of focus are: marriage preparation, marriage restoration, and marriage sustainability. We did not allow guilt and shame to condemn us because we know that our testimony is for someone else's breakthrough. Instead, we used our story to change marriages all over the world.

Made in the USA
Las Vegas, NV
20 September 2022

55654587R00098